John,

Enjoy the journey!

Praise for
The Profit Culture Formula

"In a business based on relationships, culture is critical for success. Jon and Jon provide deep insight and powerful, yet simple, ways to systematize your culture."

J. Scott Davison, *Chairman, President, & CEO, OneAmerica*

"A must-read for any leader focused on recruiting, retention, and growth."

José S. Suquet, *Chairman of the Board, President, & CEO, Pan-American Life Insurance Group*

"As a master coach to some of the country's best and most successful advisor teams, I find myself running into team culture problems all the time. Jon and Jon have lived it all, and I have watched them firsthand create one of the best cultures in the business. They know what they are doing, and the fact that they are willing to share with the rest of us is a testament to their personal desire to improve the industry. If you strive for real improvement within your team or your company, get this book, and get started. You will not regret it."

Scott Hamilton, *Certified Pareto Business Advisor*

"If you enjoy great storytelling and believe culture is the critical factor in any company's success, this is a must-read. Jon and Jon give us a fresh look at how to transform your company's culture. They definitely hit the bull's-eye!"

Susan Cooper, *Managing Director, Prudential*

"There is nothing else out there like this book! A simple road map with proven systems for any leader focused on recruiting, retention, and growth. Implement it, and your business will grow."

Brent Gritton, *Agency Vice President, One America*

"A business masterpiece with brilliant and easy-to-implement strategies that create a winning culture. It's a must for any leader focused on recruiting, retention, and growth."

Richard B. Yust, *ChfC, CLU, General Manager, Equitable Advisors*

"A must-read for any leader focused on sustainable recruiting, retention, and growth, based on Corteen and Rotter's proven, repeatable, and ongoing success."

Mark Wutt, *Vice President Sales and Distribution, Illinois Mutual*

"A fantastic read! Finally, a simple road map with proven systems to build a winning culture for any sales organization."

Marv Rotter, *Former President, Central Region Axa/Equitable*

The
PROFIT CULTURE
FORMULA

www.amplifypublishing.com

The Profit Culture Formula: The Blueprint to Successfully Recruit, Retain, and Inspire Business Professionals

©2021 Jon Corteen & Jon Rotter. All Rights Reserved. No part of this publication may be reproduced, stored in a retrieval system or transmitted in any form by any means electronic, mechanical, or photocopying, recording or otherwise without the permission of the author.

Although the author and publisher have made every effort to ensure that the information in this book was correct at press time, the author and publisher do not assume and hereby disclaim any liability to any party for any loss, damage, or disruption caused by errors or omissions, whether such errors or omissions result from negligence, accident, or any other cause.

For more information, please contact:

Amplify Publishing, an imprint of Mascot Books

620 Herndon Parkway, Suite 320

Herndon, VA 20170

info@amplifypublishing.com

Library of Congress Control Number: 2021904976

CPSIA Code: PRFRE0621A

ISBN-13: 978-1-64543-801-4

Printed in Canada

To both of our moms:
Thanks for being patient with your middle child.

The
PROFIT CULTURE
FORMULA

The Blueprint to Successfully
Recruit, Retain, and *Inspire*
Business Professionals

Jon Corteen & Jon Rotter
Co-Founders, The Culture Junky, LLC

amplify
an imprint of Mascot Books

CONTENTS

FOREWORD

This book will change your business. It will also change your perspective on life.

We all know that an organization's culture is important. At least, we give lip service to it.

But it's easier to let culture slide than to do something constructive about it.

Yet, if you ignore it, you do so at your peril. You probably know that already.

The research suggests that, globally, engagement, which is a measure of your team's buy-in to your company's mission, stands at roughly 13 percent. That means that nearly 87 percent of your people are surfing social or planning their weekend activities rather than focusing on work that moves the dial. The numbers are somewhat better in the United States, where engagement stands at about 33 percent. Still, this suggests that two-thirds of your people have very little vested interest in the long term. In contract-type environments, the numbers are even worse.

This results in lackluster performance and a never-ending revolving door of people.

Up until now, creating an engaged culture has been a black box.

The few business owners who "get it" take a very haphazard approach to it, falling into something that works for them as if by luck.

Most do not even know where to start.

Until now.

This powerful book will teach you exactly how to build a culture that fits with your very specific personality and goals; how to intentionally execute on your visionary plan; and how to create a cadence to consistently evolve it as your business grows.

Corteen and Rotter embody the phrase, "We live too much life at work to be unhappy there."

That's what it's all about. Living life!

As a leader, your own enjoyment is paramount. That's the foundation upon which intentional culture is built.

Wouldn't it be great to enjoy all seven days of the week, instead of just existing until the weekend arrives?

What if everyone in your organization felt the same way? How would that impact recruiting, retention, and, ultimately, profit?

Now, these guys built this process out of necessity.

Corteen and Rotter believe that company culture drives success. (Indeed, the evidence supports their conclusion. Every percentage increase in engagement correlates directly with revenue increase.)

This forced their hand to not just to give lip service to the concept, but to invent a solution to preserve and enhance it.

They have systematized every aspect of organizational culture.

Their twenty years of meteoric success in the financial services industry is ample proof of their accomplishments. Their unique approach to culture in the free-agent space sets them apart. Indeed, they are known for their culture, and it's not by accident.

Here's what's true: culture is way too important to leave to chance or hope.

We are all guilty of having great intentions yet falling short on execution. Life seems to always get in the way. That is when the experience suffers and culture gets ignored.

The Profit Culture Formula will bring your business and your personal agenda into perfect alignment. Nothing will slip through the cracks anymore, and you will create an organizational culture that will not only increase engagement, but will lift the bottom-line profit.

Oh, and you will be happy the entire time.

This book will change your business, your economics, and your outlook on life. But it's up to you to put the work into it. The blueprint is all here. It's detailed, it's organized, and it's easy to follow.

This book, plus a disciplined work ethic, is everything you need to reach your goals, the ones that have been eluding you for way too long.

You're holding a treasure in your hands. Dig in.

Walt Hampton, J.D.
Founder and CEO, Summit Success International
May 2021

1

YOU ARE HERE

It's a numbers game, and it sucks. You can't really fight it, because it's the way things are. There's an enemy you're up against—you're just not sure who or what it is. Maybe it's the headhunter who steals your people away. Or maybe it's the fact that nobody these days even knows what they want, and they all skip town the minute things get tough.

Bring viable bodies in, get them successful fast, and offer everyone healthy incomes. That's all you want. But you can't seem to get a foot in that revolving door.

Like you, my business peers are tired of their people jumping ship. They'll bring in recruits and no sooner than they've got them up to speed making some money, the recruits are back out the door. A fair number of those jumpers seek us out because they've heard of our culture. It's one of the reasons financial service owners bring me in to consult with them, why they sit in the audience and listen to me speak about building crazy-powerful cultures—the kind that make people stick.

We no longer see each other as competitors—my audience members and me—but as cohorts dealing with the same set of obstacles. If we can all create terrific environments, the industry wins. If we can all stop exchanging advisors like playing cards, we all stand to profit.

These are the questions they've asked me over the last dozen years: What are you doing that I'm not doing? The financial services industry has a challenging retention rate, but you've got loads of people hanging in for the long haul. You keep growing while so many others seem to be treading water or losing ground. We're doing pretty well—and plenty of them are—but what's your secret ingredient? You've got a culture like we've never seen; how do you do it?

Over cocktails and bar nuts post-conference, they try to pick my brain. They've heard me speak on stage and share my culture-building process during breakouts, but they're after the single golden nugget that's going to change the whole game for them. That's just not how it works. The pieces I can give them—and I don't mean to be cryptic— don't add up to the big picture. There are so many mindset shifts and actions that make up the whole that can't be captured with a tactic here or a practice there.

Go ahead, I want to tell them, *take one of the ideas I give you and run with it. If you don't really know why you're doing it, what's beneath it all, the transformation you're looking for will continue to evade you*. I want to help them, I really do, but until they stop looking for the quick fix, the magic blue pill, there's nothing I can do.

Now, the folks asking me questions aren't interested in culture for the sake of culture; what they're struggling with is recruiting. How do I get people in the door? That's the first thing they want to know, what they'll pay just about anything to solve. Then, they're worried about retention. How do I get them to stick, to become successful, to not get pissed off and bail in a year or two? How do I lose the burn-and-churn environment, particularly when we don't have any ownership over the people who come to work for us in our industry; when we have little leverage because they all hold their own licenses and can skip off to the next shop downtown the minute they're unhappy?

Of course, the financial service industry isn't alone when it comes to retaining free agents that spend just as much time on the phone with headhunters as they do customers and clients. When you look at any 1099 or contract-type environment—real estate or mortgage brokers, the property/casualty market, and so on—you're dealing with a group of entrepreneurs with their own mini businesses hooked up to a resource center. The only thing keeping them glued in place is their affinity for that environment, a sense of belonging, the right kind of motivators, or the lack of a better opportunity—at least for the moment. And the owners of these companies, the ones leveraging these contract workers, are blowing big money left and right trying to figure out the whole culture thing, which is just shorthand for engagement/recruitment/retention, so they can grow their own businesses and make the kind of income they know is possible. You need contractors to do that. You need them coming in the door and staying put, being pleasant to the end users who buy your services and goods. You need them to grow their businesses so you can grow yours.

When it comes to figuring out engagement and retention, however, most of us owners never stop to ask the simple question: Why would anyone be motivated to hang around?

And that's where culture comes in.

Company culture is the foundation for all things. It drives recruiting, retention, and, ultimately, profit. Most business leaders would agree that culture takes the head seat at the table when it comes to the successful future of the business, yet few companies have an implementable strategy in place to build and support an intentional culture that will drive the personality of the organization. (I'm going to come back to that word *intentional* in a bit.)

Wanting something and doing what it takes to get it, however, are two completely different things. I'm sure you'll agree.

If having a gold standard culture is critical to your business, yet you lack the implementable strategy to attain it, you have a better chance of survival fighting a bear. It may take a few years for you to bleed out, but bleed out you will. If you think stocking the fridge with Kombucha and taking the top producers to Vegas once a year is going to create the kind of loyalty that keeps folks selling for you year after year, you're sadly mistaken. Maybe I'm exaggerating here, but probably not by much.

"You've got your people talking up your company every chance they get," says my bar mate. "I know, because they're calling my people and telling them stories about how great you are, why they should join your ranks." He orders another drink: a double, no ice. He sounds exhausted. "I want to know what you're doing to create that warm-and-fuzzy." He says this as if warm-and-fuzzy were a thing.

And it is.

Culture is the average of all experiences, both the good and the bad. Our goal as owners is to eliminate the bad experiences and to not just create good experiences for our people, but to tailor them to a very specific targeted result.

You'll never have the power to pick which experiences make your culture; it will forever be the average of them all.

Here's what this guy doesn't get: Our organization, our culture, the one that all our people are bragging about, is simply a product. Culture is nothing more than a widget coming off an assembly line, a series of manufactured experiences designed with a well-thought-out end in mind. It's planned, systematized, and executed with flawless consistency.

In an *intentional* culture, the product is the client experience. (And by client, I mean the contracted advisor with whom we need to build rapport and create a mutually beneficial relationship. The person doing business in our name we want to keep around. To keep things clear, I'll refer to these people as advisors from here on.)

Nothing in our organization happens by accident. Everything is *intentional*. Everything that we do from a culture perspective, every experience we create for our people, our advisors, is *intentional*. I call them monopoly experiences, because you can't get them anywhere else. If you love these experiences and you have a craving for them, we're the only game in town to offer them. Such unique experiences aren't random, they're, that's right—*intentional*.

Absent of strategy, culture will just show up. Most of the time, this accidental culture isn't ideal or even close to what you want.

Build your product with an intended result in mind; systemize your intended experiences.

My job as the owner, as the manufacturer of an intentional culture, is to reverse engineer the assembly line to make sure that I not only build the right widget, but also keep it coming off the conveyor belt in a consistent manner.

You want a culture that your people rave about; you've got to treat it like a widget. You've got to train the assembly line workers, who serve as impact points during the manufacturing process, right down to the new advisor who calls his buddy and insists he check out your firm; you've got to have the right raw materials; and you've got to understand what you're trying to produce in the first place, and why.

Culture is a manufactured good.

I couldn't put it any simpler.

Now, you'd be mistaken to see me as cold and calculating, interested only in creating a profitable product, getting an ROI off automations. Sure, I want to run a business that makes me a ton of money, but I also want to be happy going to work. I want to like being there, around other people who like being there as well. I want people to feel like me. I want them to be excited to come to work, jump on the phone and make great connections and serious money. I want them to be just as energetic leaping out of bed on a Monday morning as they are on a Saturday. I want them just as happy to be at work as they are sitting on the couch in their living room. I want them going home to their friends and family, laughing about something someone in the office said, the fun they had, and the crazy income they see flowing their way because they're working their plan.

By the way, if you and your people don't love coming to work every day, it's your fault. Put a magnifying glass to your company culture, and the truth will be revealed. If you're not happy, then most likely the rest of the organization is miserable too. Don't think for a second that this is not impacting the bottom line. It's killing it. Happy people are productive people, and productive people are profitable people. Unhappy people cost you money, time, and energy.

That said, it's a stressful job being in the financial service industry; I can't fix that. It's a risky job, which you've got to accept coming in, whether you are an advisor or an owner. But everything else about the environment and the relationships you have with those around you, that's something you as the owner can control. That's something you can create from scratch. You have the power to make this industry, and your company so much better for everyone involved.

There is a better way. That's what this book is about.

It's time to take action and create an intentional culture where you and your people can thrive. You can't afford to put this stuff off, and I'm not simply referring to the financial cost.

Think about it. On average, half of our adult life is spent at work. If we can't have fun, if we're miserable dragging our carcass into work, then existence is one gigantic bummer. You do the math. If we live until we're eighty, we're talking forty-years-worth of crappy experiences, one after the other, with no reprieve in sight. No amount of profit makes that affliction worthwhile, not when we're given this one shot at life.

In the financial service industry, you get used to thinking and talking about death, the final destination for us all.

I got into the game straight out of college, and from day one all I did was talk about dying. Insurance plans, retirement plans—everything had mortality tied to it. It's how the math works behind the scenes. "If we start saving now versus in ten years, look how much more we'll have so that we can have enough income before we die."

Before you die, before you die. I must have said that one hundred times a day.

The clock's ticking; nothing could have been made clearer. Every day we're losing one more minute on the clock face. So, we've got to make this time allotment count.

I'm in my mid-forties now, and I look around at many of my contemporaries and see how miserable they are. Yet, they'll carry on in jobs they despise because they've got kids and a boatload of commitments. Some of them make good money, which is just one more reason they'll grin and bear it. I know what they'll do. They'll wait it out until retirement. That's when they figure they'll start enjoying life. What's the point of having a blissful retirement for five years, I ask, when, at any moment, you could get sick with cancer? Then, essentially, it's game over. Until then, they'll burn through years and years of working for the weekend, and for most of them, the weekend is only one day because Sundays are spent dreading the week ahead.

That kind of existence sucks. I know because I lived it. I was headed down that path.

For years, I was just as unhappy as my contemporaries. I'd hit the snooze button and bitch to my wife about having to get up, which is weird if you know me, because I'm normally up at 4:30 raring to go. One day, the thought of going to work practically made me sick. I couldn't face another day of managers walking the rows of cubicles like police dogs, and advisors pretending to be making calls to keep from getting in trouble. I'd been sold the entrepreneurial promise only to wind up answering to a boss. The wrong environment wasn't worth the price tag.

The thing is, I come from humble beginnings. I have more of a blue-collar mindset than you might associate with my role. No one, most of all me, ever expected for me to succeed at that level. I should've been the happiest guy in the world, but I felt wretched.

Out in the world, I looked for an opportunity that would make me happy. After a couple of failed attempts, I decided that if I couldn't find it, then I would invent it. And the rest is history.

**We live too much life at work
to be unhappy there.**

I take a sip of beer and study my peer on the next bar stool. Tailored suit, the perfect red tie, expensive haircut, manicured nails. If someone were to bet on a horse, it would be that guy, not me. I'm not the typical success story. I defied all expectations. I was the child my parents worried about winding up living in their basement. Even now, I'm no financial guru by any means. I didn't build this thing others want to dissect and imitate because I'm a really good advisor who knows product and technical aspects. I'm actually not. I guarantee the tie on the barstool knows far more about all that stuff than I do.

I'm pretty raw. I get along with a lot of folks. I used to be involved in an assortment of industry things, sit on boards, but I never knew what to do with the type who were disinclined to be real. I just decided early on to quit trying to be what I thought a financial advisor is supposed to be, and now it's just take it or leave it. This is who I am; this is how it's going be. This is how I do life.

And that's when things started accelerating for me. That's when I started attracting like-minded people who wanted nothing more than to work with and be around me. They saw what I had created for myself, and they knew it would be an oasis for them, as well.

What I'm good at is creating teams of diehard loyal fans. My business partner is, too. We find smart people who get the technical stuff, who sell enough to make us profitable and to feel successful, who stick around for years on end, who rave about the environment to their friends. We're both known for creating amazing cultures. That's why this dude is sitting here talking to me, and why dozens before him have pumped me for the very same information I'm going to share with you here.

My partner and I built a culture. Not just any culture, but the kind of culture that people call home. We figured out what it takes to create a culture that made the right people want to stay. A culture that turned them into raving fans who spread our story wide and far so we never have to worry about recruitment. A culture that made the company large amounts of money.

My bar mate checks his expensive watch. He doesn't understand why his culture sucks or why his people leave in droves. He's thrown tacos, axe-throwing competitions, and countless rounds of golf at it. He's tried, lord knows, he's tried. "All right, I guess this is who we are; this is just the way things are," he says, defeated. But then he wants to know more.

There's got to be something to this culture thing, because my partner and I are cool dudes, but we're not *that* cool. Not cool enough for people to uproot themselves over us, which is what many of our advisors had to do in order to join us. Let's face it—it's not easy to change a book of business overnight. It's actually a total pain in the ass. Our followers stood to lose clients. During a transition, they knew they wouldn't make a dime. They had to put all their plans on hold. They sacrificed all of this because that's how much they valued the culture we'd created. Even now, long after we've established ourselves in the industry, we still need to give career changers the confidence that will allow them to make a big move. We do that by providing an environment they can trust, a culture that will support them as they learn a new craft.

Build a culture like that, and a system emerges; a series of repeatable, teachable steps becomes clear. It's not that complicated, but it involves approaching the whole culture-building thing in five different stages (let's call them steps to be consistent), which we'll cover in this book:

I. **Establishing the business baseline and the bull's-eye.**

II. **Establishing your "Red Velvet Rope Rule" and acting on it.**

III. **Building the machine and turning it on.**

IV. **Attacking the gap and systematizing the plan.**

V. **Measuring growth and effectiveness; adjusting as necessary.**

If you want to create a culture that solves your recruitment, retention, growth, and income problems, this is the way we've done it. If you want to wake up excited to go to work each morning, to hang around others who are just as psyched, this is the way we've done it. If you want awesome, this is how we've done it.

Now, you can follow the traditional route, do what you've always done with the occasional stab at developing engagement or band-aiding retention, but you won't end up at awesome. You'll just end up with more of what you've got: headhunters on speed-dial, vacant-eyed advisors biding their time until a slightly better opportunity comes along, yet another chair you've got to fill, and zero growth. If you're doing well already, you can use this program to take your success to the next level.

To step away from the traditional path, however, is scary. I think we should agree about that. There's a lot at stake. You can get seriously hosed if you make the wrong move.

You may think you simply don't have time for the sort of stuff I'm about to suggest, to see recruitment (and retention, and engagement) as a selection problem. You've got hiring quotas to fill, or you can kiss your bonus goodbye. You've got a belt to tighten, what with the outrageous start-up costs of training. Your job is to bring people on so you can get them up and running fast.

Because of this, you're going to get nervous. You'll start looking around for the hammer to fall when I show you how to bring the right people into your organization, people who will thrive right from the get-go; when I show you how to determine who those people are, given the end game you have in mind; when I show you how to figure out the end game, then measure results against it; when I show you how to seek these people out; and then when I show you how to keep them happy inside of your organization, all by way of an automated system.

Because that's not the way it's been done. That's not how the industry operates or what the primer teaches.

You're going to dig your heels in when I suggest you turn away possible recruits who lack certain traits that will allow them to thrive in your environment and get rid of toxic people in your organization.

Then you're going to bump into some serious resistance when you connect with the fact that motivation isn't one-size-fits-all—when you read some of my ideas for motivating particular types and you think you must implement them all overnight. I could go on, but then you'd only wonder what you've gotten yourself into.

But here's the thing: if you take the new, narrower road, follow the steps I lay out for you without switching up the order or skipping ahead, and work the exercises and templates I give you, you'll produce the perfect culture for you and your organization. You'll get people who not only buy into you long-term, but also spread your story far and wide so everyone they know begs for a seat at your table. You'll get people who are just as thrilled as you are to come to work, who make money right along with you, who do more for you than you ever bargained.

To be clear, you may not want to replicate our culture. Not everyone will want to do it "the Corteen and Rotter way." What makes us happy may not be what makes you and your ideal people happy, and that's more than okay. We want to build you a culture that you can support because of who you are. If you borrow our culture and it's not you, it's not going to be genuine, and it's just not going to work.

I'm going to take you through all the steps, through our process, but you're going to want to put your own preferences into it. I'll show you how we think, what we put in the blanks, and the formula we were after, but you're only going to want to use it as a jumping-off point. Model it, but don't fail to make it yours.

If you implement the things that I teach you, using the same five steps we used to create the kind of culture our peers want to emulate, you'll get what you want. But this is not some shortcut to victory. You can't just use the language and change it. You can't pick and choose from the offerings, cafeteria style, and get the results you're after.

If I could emphasize one thing, it's this: your natural fear of change will no doubt get in your way. That's what's going to make you want to pull a few good ideas out of this book and abandon the rest. Ignore the planning part and jump straight into action. But the harvest you'll reap if you stick it out, if you follow the path I've laid out for you, if you refrain from skipping steps because they feel uncomfortable, irrelevant, or time-consuming, will be amazing.

There is no shortcut to victory. Sometimes it's going to feel like you're starting from scratch, and who volunteers for that? It will take time before folks start knocking at your door begging for an opportunity to work with you—which is what you want, why you're even bothering to read this book—and that's going to create some doubt. Your discipline will be tested. Some of your culture-building, engagement experiments—and those are coming—will be complete failures. Again, you'll face doubt. Peak performers, we don't like failure, so we'll cling to what we know even if it no longer serves us. Not to mention that doing things differently looks like work, and you've already got more on your plate than you can handle.

Trust me: follow the system. This is the machine that will produce the replicable widgets you actually want.

Whether you're an independent owner, a financial services manager—well, any manager—this simple five-step system will work for you. If you're an advisor operating under your own DBA, our system will work for you, too. But you must follow it, step by step.

The good news is that it's never too late to build a powerful culture. You can create an environment no one will ever want to leave, a sense of fun, and team spirit.

The bad news is that you must recover. You've got to fix your culture, or you'll get eaten alive in this highly competitive industry where choice and opportunity abound.

One final thing before we launch: You're going to need to tell yourself the truth and not just do something because someone else thinks you should, or because that's the way it's always inexplicably been done.

So, let's boot up and get to work. Right after I finish this bar mix.

Stage I

ESTABLISHING THE BASELINE AND THE BULL'S-EYE

2

THE BASELINE AND THE BULL'S-EYE

I was at another industry conference not long ago. Everybody was talking about the problems they were experiencing, and it always came back to recruiting. I can't tell you how many superficial solutions get tossed around at these events. "It would be really helpful if we could get a 25 percent discount on Career Builder. It would be more afford-able for us to get resumes," somebody will declare. I shake my head when I hear that talk. You could have a mountain of resumes on your desk, but if you have no solid culture to bring people into, well, you're never going to solve your recruitment issue. If you have no foundation, you're not going to see growth in this area or any other, because you've got nothing solid to build on. There's no story to entice newcomers or keep them around making money for you; there's nothing concrete to differentiate yourself from any other company out there. If you have a strong culture, one that your people rave about, you won't be worried about the cost of resumes. Unless I'm presenting or someone presses me for an opinion, however, I keep my mouth shut because some folks have to learn these lessons the hard way. They're not ready to hear what I've got to say because they're too focused on the painful symptoms, not the disease.

Speaking of ready, why are you reading this book? What solution are you seeking? What's the problem you mean to resolve by improving your culture? Can you put the big issue into words?

- I'm not growing fast enough: I've been doing this for ten years, and I have a firm that looks like a new start-up.
- I'm putting my heart and soul into this thing, and I'm not seeing the payoff.
- I need to make more money, or I might not be able to continue.

We're having this conversation not for the sake of culture, but because you need to solve a problem that culture can fix. If you're like most of my peers, that problem is more than likely retention or recruiting. Maybe you've identified the major issue as manpower growth. Come to think of it, you want growth not for the sake of growth, but because growth buys you revenue.

The issues are mixed up into one gigantic ball of wires, so it may seem impossible to choose just one.

Let's say you know what the problem is: You're not making enough money because you can't grow. It's all well and good to complain, but how do we measure the fact that you can't grow while you don't have enough recruiting and your retention sucks? What are the metrics that you're dealing with today that advertise this problem loud and clear? What's the linchpin—let's think of it as an indicator or two—that, if improved, will allow you to solve the problem?

Looking at the Numbers

Most of us who've been in the financial services business longer than an hour know which important numbers we need to watch if we want to stay afloat or grow. We know which indicators will speak to the health of our business or lack thereof. Most business plans include matrices that capture that information on a grid. Owners may fill them out, but then, they tend to stick them in a drawer and never look back because the documented results suck. They're pretty sure that the numbers won't change from quarter to quarter and that they'll never improve because they have no plan to move them in the right direction, so why bother?

This book is about putting together an effective culture-building plan, one that's going to do the intended job, which will be made manifest in the numbers. These numbers we're going to place on one spreadsheet, so we know where we are at all times, and why.

We need a baseline snapshot to measure improvements. That way, we can determine if the subsequent actions you take to improve your culture are moving you in the right direction and if they're fixing the specific problem you have.

Let's take this exercise step-by-step.

Exercise 2.1: Your Indicator Spreadsheet

Step 1. Gather the appropriate information and fill in the proper start columns.

Indicator	Start	Q1	Q2	Q3	Q4	% Growth (+/-) YTD
Manpower Growth						
Recruitment						
Retention						
Revenue						

Step 2. Identify the most troublesome value to target.

Maybe your retention rate is as shitty as you thought it was. (If you can't tell by looking at your starting value, you'll certainly see evidence of it at the end of the quarter.)

Now that we know how poor it is, what are you going to do about it? That's the big question. Have this troubling question rolling around in your head, and you're going to be very happy when I start making suggestions in the next few chapters ahead.

Let's see if we can get these numbers up. Let's see if we can reverse some unfortunate trends.

Most Troublesome Value = _____

Step 3. Fill in the indices' values each and every quarter.

Now, you may already be tracking these values on a quarterly basis, but I bet you're not currently associating cultural practices and events with your metrics. The question becomes: how will culture move these living indicators, and then how do we implement and systematize those practices and events that are having a positive effect on that needle? You'll know if your efforts are effective because the subsequent columns are going to tell you, loud and clear. Those values are going to be what reveals the all-important delta.

An Emphasis on Manpower Growth

You want to know what draws the most attention for me on that baseline snapshot? You may be surprised that it's not recruitment. At the end of the day, manpower is my main focus year-to-year, quarter-to-quarter. That's because manpower growth encompasses recruiting and retention, both of which have everybody all excited, and of course, total revenue. Track manpower growth, and you'll see if you're keeping advisors and if you're adding new ones. Not only that, if you dig a little deeper, you'll see interesting variations on the theme. Manpower growth will go up if you're losing advisors and adding more new people. It will stay the same if you're neither adding new people nor losing them. Each situation points to a different problem to focus on.

Now, I want to simplify the focus. At the end of the day, if you're looking to grow your manpower, you've got to attract and retain healthy, productive people, not hang on to the toxic sort just for the sake of your numbers.

Sure, you want to see your indices trend up, but not simply for the sake of winning. That's like cheating at a game of cards with your four-year-old; there's nothing in it for you.

If you have productive people in your organization and if your manpower is growing the right way, you can't help but grow your revenue (unless you're a total spazz with your expenses).

I'm all for growing manpower because if I have a hundred people doing the minimum, I know the worst-case scenario for my revenue. Sure, some of my advisors are taller and they're going to do more and they're going to raise the average, but I can predict the net result without much effort.

Frankly, I think there are too many people still trying to hunt elephants instead of focusing on growing manpower. They're all thinking, *I just gotta get that one big producer,* and that can be a really bad deal. That's how you get held hostage; that's how the elephants control your revenue. That's how they get whatever they want, or they'll leave; and then you're screwed.

If you can build manpower, you'll still have really big producers, but none of them will have you at knifepoint. If they leave, you'll be fine, because you have manpower and you'll continue to grow. Focus on that, and life will be way easier and predictable, which is why we're all here.

If you focus on manpower growth, then we can break down the indices that feed manpower growth. Then we can see where the problem is, and we can do something to affect it. We can create targets to aim for. We can test how moving this dial or that dial feeds into the equation.

Identify the Bull's-Eye

You've identified the most troublesome value to work on, the one you hope culture can fix. If, for example, you want to build a killer culture because your revenue sucks, what's your revenue right now? What did you write down?

It's all well and good to know your focus to have the baseline value established. Now it's time to decide what you'd like that number to look like in the not-too-distant future.

What do you want your revenue to be in, say, twelve months? What's the target?

I ask this because, as the old Zig Ziglar saying goes:

You can't hit a target you cannot see, and you cannot see a target you do not have.

If your current revenue is, I don't know, a million dollars, what do you want to see within this next twelve-month period? Do you want to see it grow to 1.2 million? Would that $200,000-increase be a good indication that you're going in the right direction? Could you look at that baseline revenue value you recorded and compare it to the value you put there at the end of the year and see that the actions you've taken to build culture are yielding the right results?

I'm betting your answer is yes.

If you think your issue is retention, what's your retention number right now? Do you want to double it by year's end? Would an increase of 20 percent make you jump for joy? Would it take some of the pressure off and lead you to believe that the actions you're taking to build culture are doing the trick? Would it too be a pretty good indication?

Yup.

Setting Yourself Up for the Win

Before we fill in those target values, I need to state the obvious. You're going to need to create a reasonable target to aim for, not some pie-in-the-sky nonsense. Which begs the question, what is reasonable to expect? What kind of magic can fixing your culture really create?

I'm no stranger to outlandish goals, having been around the block a few times. Apart from eye-opening personal experience, part of my job as an owner is to help my advisors establish achievable goals—SMART (Specific, Measurable, Actionable, Realistic, Time-sensitive) goals—as opposed to the pie-in-the-sky variety that sets one up for instant failure.

If there's one thing I know, it's this: You've got to get into the winning habit. If you can get into the habit of winning, you'll stop losing. Small wins establish the necessary trend to feed the winning habit. On the contrary, get in the habit of not hitting your goals, telling yourself it's okay that you didn't do what you said you were going to do in order to avoid disappointment, and you set yourself up for continual failure. You start thinking that a half-assed stab at something is good enough and wins you some conciliatory blue ribbon: nicest smile on the team, say. You stop trusting yourself to do what you claim you'll do.

The people whom I've been able to help the most—be they advisors in my firm or peers who've hired me to consult—are those who've been able to set achievable goals. They get in the habit of winning, and it hurts too much for them to lose, so they'll avoid it at all costs. And that's the point.

To determine if a goal is achievable, I have them answer three questions:

1. Can you do it?

The question goes a little deeper than that. If you've never interviewed more than two people a week, what makes you think you can interview twenty a week? What's changed? Did you suddenly fall into a huge market with tons of people just dying to talk to you? If not, we might have to go back and readjust the goal.

2. Do you know how?

Let's say you're running a five-person shop, and you'd really like to grow by two in the next year. What if you're definitely going to lose two folks because they suck, meaning you'll need to recruit four so you can grow by two? How are you going to do that? Do you (and/or your team members) need some training before you'll be able to accomplish this? Do you know what skill set you'll need in order to complete the necessary tasks to fulfill the plan?

3. What will happen if you don't?

In other words, is your "why" strong enough? Do you understand precisely what you stand to lose if you don't reach your target? Will you have to eliminate incentive bonuses if you don't make your revenue goal? Will your advisors bail on you because you've broken a promise? In other words, how will your failure trickle down? More, if you don't achieve your goal, what painful fallout will you personally have to deal with? What will it feel like to break your promises to others, let your family down, or fail to realize your fullest potential in this one-shot life? Is the very idea painful enough that you won't let it manifest no matter what?

Keep Your Eyes on Your Own Paper

I'm not going to spend much time on the idea of SMART goals, because that horse has been beaten to death. But I do want to focus on the word "realistic" for a moment.

Again, stating the obvious, what's realistic for one owner may not be realistic for another. You may be running a start-up. Or you may be an established firm with tons of people pulling in big money. Maybe you're like many of my peers with five or ten years in the business under their belts, who resemble a start-up in that they hustle every day without making much headway. Everyone is different. The needs, resources, and aims of one organization will be nothing like those of others.

I tell you this because when you fill in your target indices, you're not going to set the same goals as your neighbors—you shouldn't even want to.

When setting realistic, achievable goals, not only does size matter, personality and values do as well.

To set realistic goals, you've got to understand what matters to *you*, what makes *you* happy. Maybe you're not looking to go to the moon as an owner. I mean, you may want a six-person shop making $100,000, and you're totally cool with that. In that case, growing into a seven-person shop might be kind of neat for you; keeping your hundred grand and rolling along might be perfectly fine. The targets you set are going to be completely different from the mogul who believes that if he's not growing, he's dying. Your whole goal may be to cut your working hours down to two days a week while maintaining your manpower numbers and revenue. To do that, you'll want to figure out some efficiency to deliver that end. The mogul, he wouldn't understand why anyone would want to do that—create more time rather than money. He might want to get seven more people in during the next quarter, growing his shop to fourteen. Grow to a thirty- or forty-person shop or chase down the one-hundred-person mark, and that's when he'll be happy, feel like he's having fun.

That happiness stuff, that's what we're using culture to achieve. That happiness stuff, that's what we're going to talk about next.

Exercise 2.2: Your Target Spreadsheet

You'll want to put your target values here so you can see if you're hitting the necessary numbers, or not.

Indicator		Target Growth Q1	Target Growth Q2	Target Growth Q3	Target Growth Q4
Manpower Growth					
Recruitment					
Retention					
Revenue					

3

WHO ARE YOU, AND WHAT DO YOU WANT?

I was pulling in my driveway the other day when I noticed the all-familiar Amazon boxes on my front porch. Apparently, this was a big day. I want to talk about the "big days," when there's, like, a ten-foot-tall brown box pyramid leaning against the front door; a pyramid you can see from down the street and quite possibly from outer space. Those are the "big days" I'm talking about.

"I bet the neighbors think you have a shopping addiction," my wife said as I was dragging it all through the front door. She folded her arms across her chest and shook her head. Far less prone to order stuff off the Internet, she felt the need to ask, "Do we really need all that?"

My initial, knee-jerk guy response was, "Hell ya!" But I didn't say that because I was deathly afraid of the follow-up question: "So, what's in the boxes?" Because at that point, I couldn't remember what I'd ordered.

"Some of it falls into the need category," I said, "but most of it falls in the want category." I tried to sound smart but failed. By the way she strolled away, I knew that she knew that I knew that I was totally insane.

I stared at this sea of boxes. "So, why do I want all this stuff?" Curious, I dove into the packages like a kid on Christmas morning. The first thing I unveiled was a fishing rod.

Now, this was not my first fishing rod. In fact, I definitely had enough fishing rods that buying this one—one that admittedly cost way more than it should—automatically eliminated it from the need category. I asked myself again, "Why did I want this fishing rod?"

Then I remembered the advertisement I'd seen, and I gained instant clarity. I'd wanted it because it was constructed of the most sensitive carbon fiber ever produced in the history of the world.

And because of that, I would never miss fish again.

And because of that, I would land me an absolute monster.

And because of that, my jealous friends in the boat would have to take pics as I struggled to hold the beast up.

And because of that, I would reach fishing boat hero status.

And because of that, I could then relax and focus on the Yeti full of Coors Light in the back of the boat.

And wow, what a day, what a memory.

What an experience!

I'd wanted that fishing rod for the intended experience it was built to create for me. In fact, that's why we do most things in our lives: We chase desirable experiences. That's why I'd purchased a rod I did not need.

A profound thought occurred to me. *You know, someone else somewhere else understood that experience I'd envisioned and everything that came with it, probably right down to the Coors and the Yeti.* That person understood there were other people in the world who would be motivated by that experience and would draw enormous pleasure from it. That person understood precisely whom it would appeal to, right down to the traits that guys like me have, the very traits that would make them excited enough to click the orange "proceed with order" Amazon button. And that person created a product that would provide that experience for me and other similar buyers. This one person's idea—meant to provide a particular experience, in this case, catching a monster and becoming an absolute hero— became a product, and I became a consumer that fit the target profile.

All these thoughts swirled in my head as I stood there holding that fishing rod in the front foyer. Well, how'd that person do that? How did that person put together the perfect fishing rod that would drive someone like me to purchase it even though he had five other suitable fishing rods already in his gear closet? A rod that fit so perfectly in my hand that I contemplated taking it out for a spin before dinner. I studied the choice of carbon fiber that went into the rod and the novel way the reel was attached. The person who designed this had to love the sport the way I did. This rod spoke to challenges and pleasures only someone with personal knowledge could have understood.

I also realized it wasn't that simple, the creation process. The product required blueprints of a sort, manufacturing, and a distribution system to get that rod in front of me. Behind the rod are systems upon systems, choreographed to deliver a product that prompts an intentional experience for people just like me.

You can't just start throwing parts together willy-nilly and expect it to work like a dream; you've got to map it out so it does everything that guys like me want it to do.

Every layer in the process must be aimed at creating, with precision, the exact product that will ultimately deliver on the target experience that would interest a guy like me. Then, it's all got to roll off the back of a machine.

Now, this machine isn't fully automated. It requires human capital. So, we can't get to the output until we train the workers on the assembly line. When the machine and the people running it are executing flawlessly, then the product is produced with consistency. The ultimate experience can be delivered over and over again.

And that's when it hit me like a brown-box avalanche, why I was standing in the foyer with a fishing rod in my hand thinking about machines. A great company culture is no different. It's a manufactured product designed to appeal to a very specific type of person.

In an intentional culture, the product is the experience.

To produce this culture, you've got to start with the end in mind. You've got to understand the experience these people are after, right down to the monster fish and the hero pics, the Yeti and the Coors. You've got to paint the experience, knowing the associated pleasure it means to provide and the challenges it means to alleviate. Then you've got to map it out so it does everything that people just like you want it to do. So they'll buy it without even knowing why.

Do that, and you've got yourself a hell of a business.

Now, in the previous chapter, you identified the target result you're after in your business, be it increased revenue, or manpower growth, or something else. To hit that target, you'll need to design an intentional culture, because without one nothing will change, at least not for the better. That intentional culture, your product, will need to be blueprinted in detail. Systems will then need to be constructed to create and consistently deliver those experiences designed to wow your people. Step back and take a sweeping look at it all, and the machine reveals itself. The process, complete with all those tweaks and adjustments, parallels the manufacturing of my badass fishing rod. And like that, you've created a strategic company culture.

Like that fishing rod, your culture is going to be alluring to certain kinds of people—people who share much in common with you, who want the same experience that you do. Your culture is going to make certain people happy, just like you; others, it will leave cold, and that's just fine.

Build your product—your culture—with an intended result, deliver it to those who are equally eager to buy it, and that's how you get people to stick around and thrive, have fun, make good money, and rave about you to their friends. That's how you stay happy.

The goal now is to break down the culture you're after in very real terms and then to figure out who belongs in that environment with you, and who doesn't.

You Come First

You're the owner. So, what would you like to see when you go to work, and why? Sure, you want your culture to be comfortable so people will stick around, but you also want it to be a culture that you'll thrive in, that's suited to your personality, your style, and your take on the world. (In corporate speak, you'll hear talk of values, and while I'll use that word because it's convenient, I'm after so much more than that word connotes.)

It's okay to be selfish—100 percent selfish. You're the leader; you get to go to work, run your company, and be happy where you are. That's your inalienable right, to go all Declaration of Independence-y on you.

But, of course, that requires that you know what makes you happy. Only when you know that will you be able to figure out what kind of culture you want and the details that make up what it is you're after.

Here's the real question—well, actually, here are the real questions if you want to be grammatically correct: "Who are you, what do you want, and why? How do you want the world to be?"

Are you the guy who wants to be surrounded by snapping sharks all day because you think that's going to make you a ton of money? Do you enjoy continuously swimming and biting others too? If so, then acknowledge your sharkiness; celebrate it even. Create an environment suitable for you and your fellow hammerheads. Have an aquarium in your reception area; serve raw fish at meetings; reward your people for having sharp, white teeth and a killer instinct. Bask in your attacking, thrashing glory.

If that kind of behavior offends the hell out of you, who and what do you want instead?

Me? I want a group of people who can be around each other all day, who respect each other, the team, and the resources; who work their asses off and challenge each other; who tell the truth, even when it's hard. I want an environment of winners: people who don't accept mediocrity, people who take personal responsibility for their outcomes, and people who create their own luck. That's what rocks my world, because that's who I am as a person.

To quote Socrates, because everything in me wants to show my high school teachers that their lessons didn't necessarily fall on deaf ears:

To know thyself is the beginning of wisdom.

I'm pretty sure Socrates was stressing the need to understand your own weaknesses, but it's equally important to know your strengths and what motivates you. The more adept you become at motivating yourself, the more adept you'll be at identifying the factors that motivate others. (We're going to spend an entire chapter on motivation, so don't get ahead of me just yet.)

What's Missing Is Vision

The problem with most organizations I encounter is that nobody knows what they want, let alone who they are. They know they need culture, or they might know that their culture isn't right, or that it sucks, but they have no vision for it.

"I want a good culture," they say.

What the hell does that mean?

"I want a culture to be like one big family."

You do? I know families I don't even want to go near, who sit around the table screaming at each other and throwing shit across the room because they all hate each other. Family members who won't talk to each other, steal from each other, endlessly seek revenge, and stab each other in the back. What does "one big family" mean? Lots of hugging and campfire singing and present opening? Because both varieties of family exist.

When people say, "Hey, I want a great big family," I'm guessing that they're merely hoping that such homespun imagery will keep people around. They watched one too many *Full House* episodes when they were young. These leaders don't actually know what people want, so "family" is the closest thing they have to a glue gun. Who leaves their family, after all? (Yeah, I could name about twenty people right now.)

They have no vision, these owners, or if they do, it doesn't go deep enough.

Instead of checking some box with the "family" word, we need to get down to the nitty-gritty; we need to get intentional.

What's it like, this thing you're looking to create? What are you going for? Give me the details; give me the specifics; paint me a really clear picture, not some half-baked, stick-figure mess.

My friend, Walt, likes to use this airport analogy when he talks about the need for clarity:

"Hey, I want to go somewhere warm," a fellow says when he steps up to the ticket counter at his local airport.

"Where do you want to go?" the agent replies.

"I don't know, just somewhere warm."

Of course, the agent stares at the dude, wondering what he's supposed to plug in to his system. "Well, you could go to Florida," the agent says, trying to be helpful to everyone involved, "or you could go to California, or you could go to Hawaii—like, where do you want to go?"

Of course, without the necessary details, our traveler isn't getting off the ground, let alone getting to a place he wants to go. And without the necessary details, neither will you. (This is just another way of saying, "You can't hit a target you can't see.")

What level of detail, of specificity, am I talking about?

"I want to go to Turks and Caicos, because I know what the sand feels like on my feet, and I remember the hot sun, the way it beats down on my shoulders."

That's what I'm talking about.

I know that for a lot of you, creating a detailed picture is easier said than done.

Creating a Vision When You Have None

To get at the vision for a culture, let's look at your values as a human being, as a businessperson, first. These make for a great first layer.

Let me pause, having thrown out the word "values." Like I said, I'm not the sort who goes for corporate speak. I've attended all those defining corporate values workshops, and most of them have hurt my bald head.

Sure, there's some useful information in them, but most of that stuff I found to be a bunch of blather. So, when I use the word "values" here, take it to mean key qualities that matter to you or a suitable mindset.

If you're going to be a happy camper at work, you're going to want the people who work with you to possess a good chunk of these qualities or values or whatever we want to call them. That's why they matter.

What would you say are your top four values? (Feel free to list more if you want to.)

This is what I happen to value, what I hold as important.

1. Honor: Someone who leads with the truth, even when it's hard.
2. Personal responsibility: People who benefit from an "own it" attitude.
3. Enterprise: Entrepreneurs who create their own luck.
4. Leverage: Someone who respects resources and the team environment.

Now, it's all well and good to be able to identify your values, but we need to take this exercise one step further. You want to break each of these qualities or values down into something demonstrable—something you can pick up on in your day-to-day interactions with your people. Because the day-to-days make up the culture, the feel of the place.

For the value of honor, ask yourself the following questions:

1. If someone values honor, what kinds of things do you hear him say?
2. If someone values honor, what kinds of things do you definitely *not* hear him say?

3. If someone values honor, what kinds of things do you see him do?
4. If someone values honor, what kinds of things do you definitely *not* see him do?

I'll give you some example answers.

If someone values honor, what kinds of things do you hear him say?

1. I care about my reputation.
2. I'm all about winning the right way.
3. I can forgive an honest mistake.
4. I never say one thing and do another.

If someone values honor, what kinds of things do you not hear him say?

1. I can't trust anyone.
2. That's not fair.
3. But my intentions were good, isn't that enough?
4. Rules were made to be broken.

If someone values honor, what kinds of things do you see him do?

1. Respects others' space and privacy.
2. Corrects a mistake, even if it costs him money.
3. Puts actions to her words.
4. Puts others before himself.

If someone values honor, what kinds of things do you not see him do?

1. Undermines others to get more.
2. Reads private information.
3. Talks down to others.
4. Fails to show up as promised.

If you'd like to see how we answer these questions for our other top values, you can go to our website **theculturejunky.com/courses** and download them.

Exercise 3.1: Your Top Values

Here's an exercise for you, one that has real value (pun intended).

1. List your top four (or more) values.
2. For each of these values, answer the following questions:

   A. If someone values this, what four or five things will you hear him say?
   B. If someone values this, what four or five things will you *not* hear him say?
   C. If someone values this, what four or five things will you see him do?
   D. If someone values this, what four or five thins will you *not* see him do?

One Layer Deeper

Understanding your top values and how they present in other people is key to building a culture that will allow you to thrive. But how else can you further clarify your vision?

The following questions may seem random, but I'm going to throw them out there to get you thinking:

- What do you want your people to tell their spouse when they go home?
- How are your people integrating with each other?
- How are they supporting each other?
- What is the culture like when leadership isn't there? How might you find out?
- How are people feeling on a regular basis? Calm, stoked, resigned, or amused?

Then come at the description from this angle:

- What do you believe will change the game for your company and the people in it, knowing that both ends need to be served?
- Are you looking to create a football team where everyone competes while having fun?
- What would that look and sound like, exactly?
- Do you want a relaxed atmosphere with no apparent hierarchy?
- What, exactly, would that look and sound like?

(Want a list of additional questions to ask yourself when defining your vision? Go to **theculturejunky.com/courses**.)

You know why most leaders don't do vision exercises like these? Because they think their mission statement should cover the job. They think a candidate should be able to read the mission statement plastered on the conference room wall and appreciate the deal.

Believe me when I tell you, we're going to go so much deeper.

How are people brought into your organization and indoctrinated? That is one of the details you'll need to lock down when you're painting your picture. How are candidates shown the culture right from the get-go? That's the level of granularity to which you go. You want people to join your organization so you can boost your manpower growth and revenue; you've got to do some things to make them want to stay.

If you want to make that candidate eager to jump on board, you're not only going to need to fix your culture, you're going to need to show them what you're all about; not by embedding some crap into a nonsensical mission statement, but by telling them a terrific story.

4

SKIP THE MISSION AND VISION STATEMENTS AND TELL A BETTER STORY

Just this past week, while in the middle of writing this book, I had an interview with a young entrepreneur. She'd had some business success, wanted to integrate financial services into her offerings, and was looking to join the ranks. I liked both her enthusiasm and confidence. I could tell she was serious about the idea and had schooled herself on various business concepts and traditional interview tactics.

Late in the interview I asked, "What else can I answer for you?"

She said, "What's the mission and vision statement of the company?"

I tried not to smile. "Why is that important to you?"

She gave me what I expected, the stiff corporate answer, which basically amounted to, "Because that's how it's done in business."

"Don't take this personally," I said, "but I think those are the biggest wastes of time, energy, and mahogany on the planet." I explained that, if I walked into the lobby of 95 percent of the companies out there, grabbed the plaque off the wall, and waltzed around asking people what it meant, no one would know, including half of leadership.

Want to know what she said? "Yeah, well, that only happens when the culture's wrong."

"Exactly!"

That there is yet another example of leadership acting first, throwing darts in the fog, all before figuring out what the target is. And the worst part is this traditional bullshit has already infected the next generation. They actually think that's the glue that holds an organization together.

A Waste of Wood

Pardon me for a moment while I bore you with a definition. In general, a mission statement defines what an organization is currently doing, while a vision statement is basically the ultimate goal of what they'd like to accomplish. The mission is what people do in order to achieve the vision.

No surprises here, I'm not a huge fan of mission statements—or vision statements, for that matter—because there's zero meaning behind most of them. Like I said, they're slopped together simply because you're supposed to have one hanging on a wall or tacked up on a website in the corporate world. Most leaders can't define their mission or their vision in terms a normal human being could understand. The leaders who put them together probably haven't connected to anything they've written down. They've simply checked off the box. I'll stare at these statements and try to pick them apart like some assigned poem from tenth-grade English class, only to remain baffled. And this is the nonsense they engrave into wood, as if that does anything for them by way of differentiation, as if a potential recruit will read it and suddenly understand why he's simply *got* to work there.

What You Need Instead

I came up with a replacement for that stuff that does more to describe the vision of the culture, the one you just spent some time working on, so that you can share it with others who may want to buy in to your deal. It's called—wait for it—your story.

If you have a story, an origin story, those you tell it to will know who you are, what your take on work and life is, and why you do things the way you do.

We humans crave story, with faces we can attach to, and interesting details. (According to scientific studies, our brains light up like the Fourth of July when we read about smells, sounds, tastes, touch, and sights.) With rare exceptions, our brains simply can't retain facts and figures the same way they do a story. Nor can we attach to vague messages or corporate speak without our eyes glazing over and our brain cells shutting down. That antsy or distracted feeling you get whenever you read through dry information with very little story to ground you, that's what we call information overload. If you want someone to remember a salient point, you attach it to a story, and the information will stick like glue.

More importantly, if people like your story, they'll not only remember it, they'll also buy into it and sell it for you every chance they get. When your people love the idea of your story, when they see themselves as a fellow hero on the journey doing battle with the same villain, that's when you know you've got yourself a cultural fit. (The author

Donald Miller wrote about this very concept in his book *Building A StoryBrand: Clarify Your Message So Customers Will Listen*. It's a great book. Pick it up and read it.)

My origin story is responsible for 99 percent of my recruitment. When I sit down to talk to a candidate, I just tell my story. "Yeah," I'll say, "here's how I ended up in this room talking to you right now. Here's how I got here. Here's who I am."

Most people resonate with it right away; they've got the same story. Sure, the details are different, but it's the same experiences, feelings, hopes, and disappointments all rolled up into one.

As the story unfolds, the candidates put themselves right in the tale. They see themselves as the protagonist on the hero's journey, because they're currently living the same damn thing I did years ago. (The hero's journey, in case you're not familiar with the term, is a broad category of tale that involves a hero who goes on an adventure, and in a decisive crisis wins a victory, and then comes home changed or transformed.) These candidates just haven't gotten to the end where the situation gets better—that's why they're sitting there talking to me about a job. They listen to the experiences that I've had—the good, the bad, and the ugly—which have led me to where I am, which have formed my whole take on business and life, and they see that they're not alone. "You're the first person to put in words how I feel about my journey," they say more often the not.

My origin story becomes an oasis for them, and the company becomes a place for them to run to, a land of shared perceptions and experiences. And like that, they want in, long before we bring up compensation.

Motivation begins on day one, when we share our story, showing how the "why" for our organization is the same as the new recruit's "why," showing how the company's strategic goals are completely in line with his or hers. If a candidate has spent years and years living on the hard side enduring a reactive sales career, their eyes light up when I talk about the automated machine we've created to attain our ends and how we came to create it. That origin story is like a life ring thrown to someone whose legs are tired of treading water until the next deal comes in.

I get a lot of people to join us because they know exactly where they are, and they see it in our beginnings. They've been living their first year over and over and over, and they're tired of it, just like my partner and I were. They want a business with predictability, and that's what we do. We're all about predictability, systems, automation, and measuring ROI.

The story we tell also dramatizes our values (our mission, and our vision, too), although we don't come out and say as much. Before you can build your values into a story, by the way, you must be clear on what they are. And they must hold a charge for you, unlike the typical corporate bullshit most people spew.

See if you can pick out my values (my mission and vision, as well) in the story that follows. I'll give you a few hints.

The Origin Story I Share

I have worked both sides of the fence as the new advisor and as the manager.

I know how the bait and switch destroys people up close and personally.

When I was an advisor, I had to report to a team leader so I wouldn't get in trouble. "We're going to be your cop first, then your coach, and then your consultant," is what leaders in the industry liked to say back then, and I'm sure they still do.

I didn't want a cop. I'm an entrepreneur. I was drawn to this career because of the entrepreneurial aspect of owning my own business. I quickly found myself stuffed into an employer/employee relationship that felt like I was trapped in a box. Not the large box of ethical standards, but a small one based on other people's procedures and princi-ples. I didn't need a boss. I needed resources, support, and coaching. But try telling that to someone who was following the system. Right off the bat, I showed that I possess the enterprise value.

There I'd sit, with eight other people, making endless phone calls in my little cube. Our team leader would walk up and down outside our cubes and listen to us, just to make sure we were making our calls. I didn't have a big market when I started. I had nothing. So, I'd run out of people to call. To come up with a practical solution to the policing problem, I'd pick a kid in the office, another new agent, and we'd call each other, faking a client conversation so we wouldn't get bitched at.

I hated that practice, but there was one thing I hated even more.

Once a month, we advisors would face these huge poster boards sur-rounded by each other and our team leader. We would take out a magic marker and write our numbers down: how many phone calls we'd made, how many leads we'd gotten in other ways, and some other figures I can no longer remember. Those numbers are extremely important in the business—conversion ratios and things like that—but nobody ever taught us why. The only reason we were writing those figures down was to prove we had our numbers so we wouldn't get yelled at. We had no idea what we could use that information for.

Quotas. That's what that exercise was all about, meeting quota.

Once a month, I'd face that poster board, and it was the worst. I could feel the experience looming for the three days before. All of us hated the experience and regretted it, even the leaders.

Nothing that happened in that room ever translated to business, which was probably the biggest crime.

The team leaders said, "You just have to do this, and you'll be fine."

I spent years playing defense against leadership and whatever their plan was so I could get my own shit done. The energy required for that defense was enormous, and there's only so much energy in a day. That energy could have been better spent growing my business. Bit by bit, I pulled away from the organization instead of engaging the resources to take my business to its target, which is all I wanted. I demonstrated I valued leverage in this part of my origin story, but it had to be the right kind.

And this is how an inappropriate culture grew up around me. Fake it till you make it, or fake it till you have to bail, because it was never going to get any better. That was the way things were.

I finally looked up and said, "I'm not happy." I was making more money than I'd ever expected to make; I'd built a business and garnered a whole bunch of accolades, but none of that mattered. Only the suck mattered.

After a series of bad decisions, I finally woke up. I felt a ringing in my ears that would not go away no matter what I did. I knew in my bones it could be different. That it had to be different. There wasn't a big enough check that could be written to make me stay. In this section, I value honor as I continue to chase what I know deep down is true for me.

Luckily, I knew that we could all earn what we wanted in an environment that we wanted to be in.

Even back then I understood that this isn't a blame game. It's not about me being right and them being wrong. In fact, leadership was doing absolutely nothing wrong. Their tactics simply weren't appropriate for me. Their environment was fine; it just didn't motivate me to be my best. This part of my story is all about personal responsibility and not playing the blame game.

I made a couple of moves, looking for what it was that I was after. I couldn't find it, so I had to invent it.

Now I'm the boss. I'm the leader, the manager. Truth is, I never wanted to be the boss, not in the traditional sense, particularly for people who, like me, don't need a boss. I'm not interested in micromanaging. If I don't see someone for five days, I don't care. I care about the person, sure, but it's not my business—it belongs to them. I'm not going to tell anyone what time to get out of bed, what time to get their ass into the office, or what time they leave. They're adults, business owners, entrepreneurs—they can decide that for themselves without my help.

Most of my peers would recoil at the notion that I don't keep track of advisors' comings and goings. I don't dictate how they spend their days. They'll have time enough to prove their worth in action, to make it clear that they deserve for me to partner with them in their business. But I've got to tell you, I chose to flip the whole boss–employee relationship thing on its head, because, for people like me, the dynamic I'd experienced before left me cold. Work-life, the temperature of the office, the culture, how it feels to be a part of an organization, that there will make or break a person—and the business they're a part of.

No one comes to work for this company. I'm not going to be your boss, or anybody else's. I'm bringing the resources, the coaching, the education, and the leverage, but we're going to custom-tailor it to your plan and where you want to go. Because you're not going to do much of anything because I said you should, unless I'm chasing you with a stick and threatening you, which I have no interest in doing. If you have this mega carrot out there that you're chasing, a carrot of your own choosing, you're going to run it down and eat it. You'll get up every day and go for it if you're truly an entrepreneur, truly a business owner.

And that's what I'm interested in bringing into my company, into my culture. Entrepreneurs. Because they're the people who're going to thrive in the environment I've created. I'm an entrepreneur. I want nothing more than to be surrounded by other entrepreneurs. Professionally, I don't relate to nine-to-fivers because we're hardwired so differently. Through no fault of their own, they would find my entrepreneurial culture totally unsuitable, which is cool.

When we started building our culture, my partner and I were crystal-clear about the kind of people we thought would thrive in our risk-intensive industry. Of course, we looked to our previous experiences and knew we needed people like us.

What environment works for entrepreneurs? we asked ourselves. *If we were to create a culture from scratch, what things would we have to consider that weren't necessarily obvious on the first pass?*

In the process, we pinpointed two foundational cornerstones we knew we had to put in place and adhere to.

If we wanted to keep an entrepreneur happy, the first thing we had to do was get rid of that godawful box we'd been forced to operate in. Smash it, burn it, toss it out, never let it back in. Instead of working for a company, our folks would feel like the firm had partnered with them in their business.

We respected the phrase that there's always a plan in place; it's either yours, or you're a part of someone else's. Our focus, however, was to make it all about our advisor's plan, then to create experiences that prove that they've aligned with a firm that embraces their motivation and their target.

The second was to redefine our firm's client. The whole key to creating a dynamic that would work for everyone involved and would keep entrepreneurial types hanging around came to me in a flash. We had to change our definition of client. Not just give it lip service, because, come on, we've heard this new client definition a thousand times before—but live it.

Our client at the firm is not the end user—the customer who buys a financial product—because there's no relationship there. That relationship—and we all know it's an important one—is covered by the advisor.

The advisor is the face of the business as far as the end user is concerned. It's the advisor who builds rapport, who excavates the deeper needs and fears, researches the solutions, and creates a suitable action plan based on the data. That end user is the advisor's client, plain and simple.

No, our client is the advisor.

No different than how an advisor customizes a plan for his or her client, we had to do the same with ours. A one-size-fits-all plan, a hey-this-is-just-how-it's-done approach was the very thing that had to go. If we approached advisors the way they do the end-user—getting to know their individual needs, coming up with relevant solutions, putting together an individualized action plan based on the data—think how valued and seen they'd feel.

As the leader, why shouldn't I sit down with an advisor who's just joined our firm and find out everything I can about them? Instead of asking them about their vision for retirement—When are you seeing it? What does it feel like? What are you doing?—I'd go after the vision they have for their career. Where are they trying to go? What's been getting in the way thus far? What do their big dreams and desires feel like? What do they look like, sound like, taste like? Closing the gap on the timeline, I'd ask, "Where do you need to be in two years? What's it like there? What are you doing? What needs to happen by way of success so you can look back and say, 'I'm damn glad I met that bald Corteen dude and made a confident change in my life?'" I want to know how this person wants to spend his time. Why? In other words, I want to know what motivates him.

Thinking like an advisor, I considered the second piece. After asking a new hire all those questions, deriving all the hard and soft data, then it's time to come back to them with my resources, my technology, a working plan. "You know what? I have a lot of advisors who are similar to you, but they're not exactly like you, so this is a very unique customized solution for your situation. Follow this, and you're already on a better track. This will work for you, now it's time for you to go build it."

What happens when we engage with advisors this way? We feel awesome, we make a bunch of money, and we've put advisors in a far better place. That's what gets us up in the morning in the industry. That's what we strive to do.

To that end, my partner and I came up with a menu of opportunities and resources an advisor could plug into as needed based on their own direction and plan.

Moreover, we knew it was absolutely critical that we create a web of motivation that could capture the vast array of our clientele we refer to as advisors. Sure, our advisors have a lot in common, and yet their motivation styles differ. (We'll address motivation styles in Chapter 9.) When new advisors come on, they're shocked when we spend a whole bunch of time determining just what rocks their world. It clicks in that they're someplace they've never been before.

Like I said, I'm not the kind of guy who's going to run around with a stick and tell them, "Do this or else." So what I had to do is build the biggest bag of carrots and offer them up. One carrot might motivate this kind of person. One carrot might motivate that kind. This carrot might motivate five people. All of the carrots might motivate one person. But I've got to cast a wide net, because I've got all different types of people from a motivational standpoint who fit in our culture. I have to make sure that I'm doing things in each of these areas consistently so that my net is wide enough to can capture everybody. Systematically addressing all forms of motivation in a consistent manner drives tremendous results.

If we truly recognize and support the plan of our advisor and their entrepreneurial spirit, then traditional management, the kind that comes armed with the stick, is nothing but counterproductive. We deal in carrots, not sticks.

We threw away the regular playbook, sticks included, because the old way of doing things would never serve our end. We vowed to put everything we had into our advisors, into the relationships we had with them, and our shared experiences.

Our whole goal was to create an environment where people could make money and have fun going to work as opposed to, "Oh my god, I gotta show up there at eight o'clock on Monday, and please, please let me get through to Friday." When you're having fun, when everyone's having fun together, it makes the experience 1,000 times better for all involved, including "the boss."

When everybody else is excited, then I get excited.

The end game is a culture unlike anything else. Something we're proud to call a "Monopoly Culture" because you can't get it anywhere else. Once you experience its gravity, a craving develops, and all other options disappear. Quickly, we become the only game in town for our advisors because the only place to get that experience is here.

What happens when we do this with our advisors? They not only hang around, they prosper—and so do we.

Developing Your Origin Story

That story I just told you allows me to connect with most people I get in front of me, because each individual can connect with a different part of that hero's journey. The other day, for instance, I was interviewing a sophisticated woman a dozen years older than I am. On the surface, we couldn't be more different. At the end of my story, she said, "Wow, we have so much in common. I feel like we lived the same life."

That's the power of a well-told story—more accurately, a well-constructed story.

Now, it's time we came up with yours, because, try as you might, my story will not work for you. I can promise you that.

What's your unique story?

Where do you come from?

Who are you?

What do you stand for?

What obstacles have you overcome on your climb up the ladder?

What dragons have you had to slay?

How did your journey change you?

What makes your struggle universal?

What makes it unique to you?

That story you share with others is the "why" behind what you're doing and why you're going to continue doing what you're doing. Your origin story, your company origin story, which, of course, can't be separated from who you are as a person, dramatizes your deepest values.

Your origin story as the owner, as the leader, sets the entire tone for the organization. It spells out who you're going to relate to, who's going to relate to you, who's going to be a fit, who's not, and why.

We express these values in story form, first of all because stories are what hold interest and make things real for the listener, but also because they help listeners decide if they share the same values in a casual, conversational way. It's just a story. The story either resonates with them, or it doesn't. No harm, no foul.

Your story is the basis of your culture. It needs to be one that others can connect to, get excited about, and inspire them to share it with the world. A dynamic story is the most powerful internal and external marketing tool you have.

Still, you'd be surprised how many leaders get their origin story wrong.

Sometimes the story they tell feels remarkably uninspiring because the value system is vague or completely missing. (See why I took you through that value exercise?) And sometimes the story falls off the tracks because it lacks one or more crucial elements.

Ever wonder what makes a makes a movie a blockbuster, or a series binge worthy? Simply put, the story connects with a ton of folks. Those stories have a certain blueprint to them that connects them to the broadest audience, and it works every time. Understanding and accepting this would make it futile not to incorporate this same structure behind our own story.

So let's dig into that . . .

The Elements of a Good Story

Remember, there's an art to writing and telling a story, which you may have learned in freshman English class and, like me, summarily forgot. This is why I'm going to give you a roadmap for the creation of one.

The basic elements of story are traditionally considered to be, plot, character, setting, theme, and conflict.

A good origin story contains these components:

1. Plot

Plot is your foundation. Most people think of plot as a chain of events that take place, but there's much more to it than that. A good plot has conflict and a satisfying resolution. The main character—also known as the protagonist or the hero—must be challenged in some way. They can't be wandering around smelling flowers or chatting with co-workers, or he or she wouldn't be on a hero's journey. That tension-filled journey has a classic shape: The rising action is the beginning of the conflict, the apex is the intense turning point, within the falling action the hero begins to resolve the conflict, and the final act brings us to the resolution where we are today. There's an arc to the plot, to the story, waypoints you have to hit if you want your audience member to stick around long enough to see what happens. We need lots of dramatic tension.

2. Character

Characters are the players, the actors in your story, including the hero/protagonist. There's usually an antagonist or two as well—someone who creates problems for the hero and complicates life. Often, these players, and the other supporting cast, combine to create a community, one in which great things (or horrible things) are built. Showcasing unique individuals tied to the common belief or goal will highlight diversity and dramatize a culture of acceptance and collaboration.

3. Setting

The setting is the place, environment, and even era where the action takes place. The setting is where the characters and the plot come together. Not only are you initiating the time and the place of the story with your chosen setting, but you're also creating the mood with some well-chosen details. It's critical that your audience connect with the mood as it applies to each and every plot point.

4. Theme

The theme binds all of the elements into a smooth story. This is the ultimate message that you want your audience to walk away with. It's the ah-ha moment when your audience experiences a full understanding of what you are all about.

5. Conflict

Conflict is the struggle between two forces. The external variety occurs outside of a character, while the internal variety occurs within one character. Every story has a conflict to solve. The plot is centered on this conflict and the ways in which the characters attempt to resolve the problem.

If you can identify these elements on the page, you can model them.

If you were to study my origin story, you could pick out the following:

1. **The plot (and the plot points)**: Jon the entrepreneur finds himself trapped in a box with no way out. He breaks out to create a workplace environment in which he can be happy. He and his partner design a culture, which attracts other people just like them.
2. **The characters**: Jon is the hero of the story, as is his partner. The antagonist: his former leadership. The community is composed of like-minded entrepreneurs who want nothing more than to escape the box and to be aided by servant leaders.
3. **The setting**: We move from a bygone era of tiny cubicles guarded by whip-snapping team leaders and a conference room with a list of names and numbers on a whiteboard, to a fun racetrack baited with fast-moving motivational carrots.
4. **The theme**: Entrepreneurs don't need a boss, but they want a bunch of other stuff. They want coaching, resources, leverage, and education, just to name a few. They need an individualized

plan and the right kind of motivation in order to make money and be happy.

5. **The conflict:** External conflict arises when Jon must fight the leadership forces that want to tell him what to do. Internal conflict abounds within Jon, because he's told he should be happy and productive, but he's not. Something may be off, and it could be him.

Do you see why your origin story is vastly different from a mission statement? I mean, night and day, right?

The next thing you want to do is:

Exercise 4.1: Write Your Origin Story

Make sure your story includes your values and each of the five elements I just described. (Look, if you could spend all that time putting together an indecipherable mission statement, you can spend some time doing this.)

Your top 4 core values	
Sketch of plot with at least 4 plot points	
Main characters including hero(s) & antagonist(s)	
Description of setting(s) including era	
Theme, takeaway message that sums up your whole deal	
Conflict. Who/what is getting in the way. Internal/external obstacles	

Your Story Template

Fill in the spaces so you have starting material to work with. You know what you'll need to include when you begin writing your first draft. Trust me, this story will not fall out of your mouth just because you'd like it to. You need to spend some time working it until you've got something that will flow.

Now, take this material and tell us something that's going to make us want to throw all caution to the wind in order to join your ranks.

Here's the takeaway to this whole writing lesson: to tell a good story, one that will draw recruits to you like metal filings to a magnet, you've got to have the vision, and you've got to know why you have that vision. Tell us why you want that stuff within your origin story.

No doubt you can do it the Corteen way. I'm giving you the template and the process I used so that you could build your own story, one that magnetizes the right people. But I'm going to repeat myself for the millionth time: what makes me happy is not going to necessarily make you happy. A culture that I can support because of who I am doesn't mean that it can support you. It doesn't make it the right target for you. Your culture has to be a genuine fit for you, or it's just not going to work. You'll be as indifferent to it as my buddy is to that wonderful new fishing rod I bought off Amazon. Insert your own values and sensibilities for your own sake.

Some people don't want true entrepreneurs in their business; we've established that. They may claim they do, particularly when recruiting and singing out of the standard hymnbook, but they're not set up to handle folks like that. And that's okay. You don't need to create a carbon copy of my culture, because you're a different person. You may want compliant nine-to-fivers who need a manager to keep them moving. And there are plenty of folks out there who want and need that kind of setting, who better envision a productive and invigorating future as part of another's plan. They wouldn't thrive in an entrepreneurial environment because that's not who they are, but a heavily monitored setting, that's right where they belong. The ability to win is all about appropriateness of the environment for a given person.

Now, let's figure out how we can identify those that match, pulling them from the masses so we can bring them into the fold. While we're doing that, let's figure out who would make for a miserable fit so we can politely show them the door.

Stage II

ESTABLISHING YOUR "RED VELVET ROPE RULE" AND ACTING ON IT

5

DEFINE YOUR RED VELVET ROPE RULE

I see recruitment (and retention, and engagement) as a selection problem. Well, let me clarify that statement: poor selection is the first part of the problem; poor execution the other. There are two reasons people fail with us. One is that we select somebody who shouldn't be brought in-house in the first place. The second is that we fail to deliver everything we promised. And the second one is inexcusable.

The front end. That's where change is really going to be made. That's why I'm beginning the chapter this way.

A couple of things happen when I approach the topic of recruitment with leaders and owners in my industry. First, they get really nervous when I use the word "selective." You can be selective about your beer brand, or the kind of gas you put in your car, but don't start down that path when it comes to new recruits, particularly those pirated from other agencies or snagged by headhunters. Many of my peers have hiring quotas they need to fill, or they can kiss their bonuses goodbye.

If they start peeling semi-viable human beings off the top of the pile, they're not taking their family anywhere for summer vacation. They've got a belt to tighten, what with the outrageous start-up costs of training, so they don't want to hear about anything new that could interrupt their feng shui. Their job is to bring people on, get them up and running fast, and rotate them into the mix.

"If I'm turning someone around and showing him the door, where's the next candidate coming from?" That's the question they're asking, out loud or otherwise.

Truth be told, most owners I know don't have enough activity in the recruiting side. They're not interviewing, or if they are, they aren't getting past the first interview. They're heavily dependent on cold sources and purchased resumes. They blame the problem on resumes, but they also get the need to improve their culture so they have something to recruit into. They're open to culture being the solution; they just don't trust the required process quite yet.

Now, I'm sure many of my peers have hiring standards in place as part of their selection process, separate and apart from the industry requirements that need to be ticked off, including licensure and proof of a clean background check. They also make use of some of the common industry tools that assess a candidate's potential survival. So, it's not like they'll pull just anyone off the streets and offer to bring them in house—there are hurdles involved. Beyond this, however, I'm guessing that most base their hiring decisions on just a gut check, which is what my partner and I always did before we had a system.

As I said, on whole, the industry has a very low retention rate, one that isn't far off from most small business startups. "Why is this so low?" asks every leader I've ever met. I've got the answer, but not everyone wants to hear it: if we treated recruitment the right way, if we brought in the right people, we could raise that rate, no problem.

There's a perfectly good reason my answer would fall on deaf ears. My peers are convinced the hiring pool has gotten ridiculously small.

Fewer and fewer new people are brought into this industry each year because the start-up costs of training and getting newbies up to speed are way too high, particularly in light of the fact that most tend to bail after a year or two. Most owners have stepped away from trying to raise somebody new; their whole goal is to get industry-experienced people to save them the hundred grand or so. Because of this, they're all running around in the industry stealing everybody else's people.

With a lack of fresh blood, the average age of a financial advisor is now (as of this writing) in the late fifties, and they're getting older every year. We're talking about folks who routinely jump from ship to ship because they've yet to find a place they consider "home." That's whom my peers are trying to recruit from one another without any eye on selectivity.

The few peers who are trying to pull from colleges and the career transition pond, not just snag industry vets, tend to miss this key element: targeting and systematizing selection based on their cultural criteria.

Here's why that matters.

While other owners are trying to stick a foot in this revolving door or beat the same bushes everyone else is, I get most of my hires through the people who already work in our organization.

Recently, I had a woman come in for her first day on the job. Her friend, another young newcomer with no industry experience, had called her the month before. "You've gotta get over here and meet these people. This place is fantastic!"

That there is how we do most of our hiring. One of our advisors falls in love with our culture because she's a total match, and before long, she's spreading the word near and far. She's diving into her pool of like-minded people and hauling them in. She can spot the fit before we can. Our current advisors are guarding the door, letting in only those who promise to do well. Our hiring, in other words, is all culture driven.

I should note that many in the industry currently have agent referral programs and incentives in place. The concept isn't novel. And yet, these programs yield little if any results because there's no culture to back them. Maybe owners bring in a few new hires that way, but without an intentional culture to attach to, they don't keep them for very long.

While our current advisors have a good intuitive feel about fit, they've also been told in no uncertain terms whom we're looking to attract. They've been schooled on our Red Velvet Rope Rule, and they value the fact that we're something of an exclusive club.

Let me explain.

Creating Your Red Velvet Rope

Michael Port of *Book Yourself Solid* fame tells the following story: Imagine that your buddy has invited you to accompany him to an invitation-only special event. You arrive, dressed to the nines, and are surprised to find a red velvet rope stretched between two shiny brass poles at the entrance. A man in a top hat asks your name, checking his invitation list. Finding your name there, he flashes a smile and drops one end of the rope, allowing you into the party. You feel like a rock star. That's how you feel when you get in knowing that others don't.

Now, here's the question: when it comes to your business, do you have your own Red Velvet Rope Rule that allows in only the most ideal advisors, the ones who energize and inspire you? The ones who would fit in nicely to the culture you've just spent all that time describing, right down to what you hear people saying in the hall and what they do in their time off? Or do you let in anyone with a pulse and a license simply because you need all the butts in chairs you can get?

If you don't have a Red Velvet Rope Rule yet, you will shortly.

Why?

First, because when you work with advisors you love, you'll truly enjoy the work you're doing; you'll love every minute of it, which, if you remember right, is a big part of the goal. And when you love every minute of the work you do, you'll do your best work, which means you'll make real money.

Second, because you *are* your advisors. Your advisors are an expression and an extension of you, be you a shark or the entrepreneurial type or a micromanager. You are the company you keep. Choose your advisors as carefully as you choose your friends. Actually, choose them more carefully, because it's safe to assume that many of your advisors will become your friends.

Now, I need folks with CEO mentalities because, remember, I'm not into micromanaging. It's just not who I am as a person. Much of my Red Velvet Rope Rule is built around this very important fact.

Right from the get-go, I knew that the people I was looking to bring into my organization had to drive the car; they had to work the gas pedal and the brake; they had to steer. Me? My intention was (and is) to jump in the passenger seat with the GPS. I was the one who helped my advisors find shortcuts and get around traffic. I was the one bringing the resources, telling them where the gas stations were so they wouldn't run out of fuel before they got to their destination. I was the one who jacked the wheel if they were about to go into a ditch because they'd fallen asleep. That was the symbiotic relationship I meant to create from day one. The people I was looking for—and continue to look for—had to want that kind of interaction.

I needed self-managers, entrepreneurs, which is precisely who I went out to recruit.

Let me back up for a moment.

Before we began the recruiting process, my partner and I stood before a whiteboard and began to dissect how to identify real entrepreneurs. We got crystal-clear on precisely what these people were made up of.

We also described the tip-offs that told us we were dealing with anything but.

Does this process sound familiar? It should. You went through this very questioning process when you were putting together your culture vision.

When you know the general feel and energy you're after with your culture, then you need to hone in on the details of the people who would fit this ideal.

If I want an environment and culture in which we all—interdependently—drive to the economic finish line every single day, then I've got to figure out how to bring in people who share that desire. I've got to figure out how to select them from the pool of recruits who knock at my door. But here's the good news: the type of people we were after wouldn't just look and sound different; they'd respond to certain stimuli, and not to others.

A Red Velvet Rope vs. The Ideal Candidate Profile

Whenever I mention "the ideal candidate profile," to use industry terms, most of my peers immediately head to our standard industry assessment. "What did they score?" they want to know when talking about a potential recruit. "How did they do?" "What kind of income did they earn at their last job?" "How many clients did they have?" (By the way, these are all relevant questions.)

The specific profile that will suit our needs requires that we evolve the criteria we're looking for in people.

What do I mean?

Well, they've got to be fun, these candidates; that's just one of my criteria. They just have to be fun. If we're not laughing in that meeting, I'm out. And trust me, there's nothing on a standardized assessment that will tell me that.

We need to dig deeper. Not only do we have to determine what we're specifically after in candidates and why, we've got to spend some time fact-finding and having real conversations with them so we can get at their true essence and determine the fit. Like everything we do, there is a process that we follow to that end.

My Red Velvet Rope Process

During our opening interviews, I set the agenda straight with the candidate. "Look, we're going to figure out today if we can be in a room together and if we actually enjoy it, and then we'll get into the details. This is not a compensation conversation. I've got to be able to see you and be excited to help you, and you've got to be able to see me and be excited to be part of this organization, first. Then, we'll get to the details."

I take the whole evaluation of a candidate in steps; that's just how my mind works.

Number one: are they right for this industry? That's what I'm asking myself at the very beginning. I bring in a ton of candidates with no prior experience. That means I've got to dig into things like sales mentality. Can they engage with people? Are they just going to stand in the corner and avoid talking to people? There are certain industry requirements that need to be considered, no ifs, ands, or buts: you have to be able to create relationships and engage with others. If they don't have this stuff, they're out.

The second question I'm asking myself is: are they ready for our platform? Can we support everything they want to do and where they want to go, or do their requirements fall outside of that? If so, no one's going to be happy, so I refer him or her somewhere else.

Third and most important is: are they right for the culture? Can we make them better? Can they make us better?

That's where the artistry comes in. This is where our initial design process kicks in. We've spent a lot of time figuring out who is a fit for us and who isn't. We've determined the attributes a person needs to have to flourish in our culture and which would be fatal to the whole. From that work, our Red Velvet Rope Rule was born.

Our Red Velvet Rope Rule has also evolved with experience. Yes, we know what kind of people are going to mesh with us, with the environment and culture we wish to create, but we have a long history, as well. We know the sorts of people who have thrived, survived, and bombed. We can describe each type to a T.

Champions

My team and I are always on the lookout for the next champion advisor: the advisor who's a blast to work with and can totally blow us out of the water. We're looking and listening for key qualities. We watch, and we pay attention to what's being said at every juncture.

If I were to describe our champion advisors, their ethics, what they talk about, how they contribute to society, what they like to do, their qualities, who they hang around, this is how we might begin:

I met Greg when he was seventeen years in the business. At that point, I would have described him as a reactive salesperson as opposed to a business owner. He was making decent money but nothing near his potential.

He was clearly a road warrior, someone who put his heart and soul into the business, because he'd ring from different states. "I'm in Illinois," he'd say, "and now I've got a meeting in Wisconsin, and then I'm going to Indiana." I was like, "Jeez, do you have a helicopter or what?" Guy just kills himself for it.

One night, I said, "Greg, I think you might be missing a zero from your income." He dismissed my statement out of hand. Yet, the next morning, there he was in my office. He wanted to know why I'd said what I said. I replied, "I don't know anybody who's more passionate about what he's doing or who works as hard as you do. But look at the return that you're getting and the sacrifices you're making. You could have a different quality of life."

He saw a glimmer of truth to the statement, so he allowed me to coach him.

Bit by bit, Greg began to see his true value. Some people, by the way, never make that leap. "On this planet, what are you worth?" That's a hard question for people to answer. But Greg suddenly realized he was worth a helluva lot more than his current paycheck.

We'd sit down once a week and talk stuff through. "Where do you want to go?" I'd ask him. We'd talk for hours, side by side, in order to clarify the picture.

I hired Greg because he possessed honor, personal responsibility, and enterprise, and he appreciated leverage. He'd respect our resources and the team environment. I just knew he'd thrive in our ecosystem. The thing is, Greg was in this industry for seventeen years with those four traits. He'd had them since he was born. In a different environment, those four traits hadn't taken him to the moon. He didn't soar.

He's got his own machine now, complete with employees and partners. He's very, very humble, and he knows how he got to his current situation—that it wasn't by himself. He's a true team player.

What Greg was willing to do was listen and take a chance. We do well with people who can adopt some risk in their lives.

Over the years, I watched Greg tear it up. He would get up in the morning and just hammer it out. Now, after paying his dues, he gets to eat dinner at home. But I remember when things really began taking off for him. "I just took my first vacation," he said. When I looked surprised, he said, "Seriously. I just took my first vacation. Normally, when we go away, I work the whole time. But this time, I didn't work, and I still made money."

There's nothing more satisfying than seeing how I helped him change his life. I'm not into bragging. I'm saying this because culture isn't just about making more money. It's about having impact. It's about happiness and joy.

Greg and his family have upgraded their lifestyle. They're doing all this cool stuff. They're sending their kids to great schools. That's just so rewarding. Greg has won our top honor multiple times, and his speech never lacks tribute to the environment and the experiences that have impacted his game-changing success. Greg is one of our biggest cheerleaders. He has tremendous respect for what we do and how we do it.

Recently, we sat together planning for the next quarter. "I can't believe that these numbers are next to my name," he said. "It's weird. It's actually uncomfortable."

"Well, it's the number that should've been there the whole time," I said, "And it's time to set the next target." And, boom, he accepted the statement without question.

We have a great cadence going, Greg and I. He doesn't miss a meeting. He never feels like he's done, and he keeps his eye on the next horizon, understanding that the target will bring opportunity as well as fresh obstacles.

Champion Qualities I Look For

I'm certain that, having read what it is that I value in Chapter 3, none of these superstar qualities will surprise you:

1. An enterprising mindset
2. Honor and respect for the truth, even when the truth is hard
3. Acceptance of personal responsibility for his or her destiny
4. Value of resources and the team environment

Exercise 5.1: Define Your Champions

List the qualities, values, and personal characteristics that will fit with your culture.

If you'd like a template to help organize your thoughts, you can download one at **theculturejunky.com/courses**.

Kryptonite

Now, just as you can spot champion qualities and traits, you can also pick up on warning signs. Most of us have been privy to conversations studded with threats of ethical violations. We've picked up on comments, overt or subtle in nature, that makes us think, *Oh shit, no way.* But rare is the leader who's defined cultural Kryptonite with pen and paper, what it actually looks and sounds like in living color. And without this clear picture, you'd be surprised what makes it past your Red Velvet Rope only to wreak havoc.

Or maybe you wouldn't be surprised because, given the recruitment numbers you may be trying to hit, if a complainer is breathing, he's probably been allowed in. I mention complainers, because, if ever there were cultural Kryptonite for us, it would be a complainer.

I'm always amazed when I'm sitting across from complainers. You know the type: it's just everybody else's fault all the freaking time. They just happen to always work for the worst people in the world, whose number one goal in life is to sabotage them. Even if it's 85° F and sunny, the weather sucks because it's too hot. If it's 65° F outside and shady, then they can't understand why we all don't just pick up and move to Florida. I can't imagine how they've managed to worm their way into any organization that requires people skills. Those are short meetings. Very, very short. I can't have that kind of person in my environment.

Complainers are easy enough to spot, but it takes a practiced ear to pick up on the qualities and values we're out to avoid. Let me correct myself: it takes brainstorming to come up with a clear description of Kryptonite in its various guises.

Let's say one of your top values is contribution. (It rates pretty high on our list, as well.) That's not nearly as easy to pick up on in conversation, which means we need to intentionally describe what that looks like and what it doesn't.

For example, it's all well and good that someone volunteers for a board or a community project. On the surface, that looks like it would connect with the contribution value. But some people do that stuff because they think they're supposed to, or they think it sounds good coming out of their mouths. People like that, well, they're the opposite of what I think of when I use the word contribution.

I'm far more interested in understanding how candidates spend their time in general, as opposed to fixating on their memberships and associations. If some candidate is a member of some big, impressive organization and another one goes home every single day to help his little brother learn his soccer skills, which one's better? Who cares the most? Who's the most engaged? I don't know, probably the dude who's helping his little brother. However, if someone goes home every night and plays video games, if he isolates himself and never hangs out with his buddies, then chances are really good that he doesn't value contribution (or community), and he'll fail to fit into our organization. That's Kryptonite as far as we're concerned.

Remember, our culture is perfect for entrepreneurs. That means the risk-averse type will never thrive in what we've created.

Before I go on, let me say something about those on-the-safe-path employees, so you know where I'm coming from. My older brother and I, we're very much alike. We even look like each other. He's an engineer, and has wanted to be one since he was, like, two. He's successful and brilliant and super hard working, and he likes the certainty of a salary. He looks at me and says, "I don't know how you sleep at night with all the risks that you take." (See, I don't even notice the risk, people like me generally don't.)

I could move in with my brother, and, try as I might, I couldn't get him to have an entrepreneurial mindset with all the inherent risk any more than he could turn me into a safe-path dude who answers to a boss. It's just not going to happen no matter what. Plain and simple, I would die in his world, and he would die in mine.

So again, we're talking about matchmaking. That's all we're trying to do here. That's why we're looking for these traits.

So, how do we pick out the risk-averse type before they slip under our Red Velvet Rope? What do they look like and sound like, even when they know how to talk it up?

A dead giveaway is the inability to tolerate any sort of risk, first and foremost. I'll dig into that line of questioning like a terrier. I want to find places in a candidate's life where she took a risk and did so multiple times. If I hear anything along the lines of, "I didn't take risks, not once, and if I fail, I'm out of there," well, *I'm* out of there.

To fit in my culture, you've got to approach risk as something you've got to drive straight to the finish line. That's the game.

I'm big on the "why" side of life—that's where I dig in when I'm talking to a candidate. That's where I get picky. When I start poking into the "why," that's when I see the tears. That's when I understand who is going to kill themselves before they fail and who will get up and simply look for another job.

Other Kryptonite Qualities I Look For

Again, none of this should surprise you by now.

1. Dishonest
2. Takes all the credit
3. Lone wolf vs. team player
4. The inability to laugh or lighten up

Exercise 5.2: Define Your Kryptonite

List the qualities, values, personal characteristics that will clash with your culture.

If you'd like to a template to help organize your thoughts, you can download one at **theculturejunky.com/courses**.

Here's the scoop: your organization can be composed of people of varying temperaments. Not everyone has to be a carbon copy of you. My partner and I have an extremely diverse group working with us. We're diverse in terms of race, religion, ethnic background—you name it. But where we're not diverse in our organization is our core traits. We all share those. And that's why it works. That's where our power comes from. Diversity on the outside, matched with a uniformity of values that holds us all together on the inside.

To have this same power, you need to understand the big picture and narrow in on the details. That's how you'll see cultural change. You need to understand what your next Champion looks like when you're sitting across from her. You need to be able to tell who smells like Kryptonite from moment one so you never let him in the door.

Of course, between those major benchmarks lies a lot of in-between. Those who pass your Red Velvet Rope Rule should, however, have the core qualities you've defined. They should share a similar energy; say a certain level of what some may see as volatility, others as high energy and passion. They should have a comparable ability to deal with stress. They should share qualities—leadership perhaps among them—all of which feed the culture you intend.

Evaluating the Current Gene Pool

Now it's time to address the current members of your organization, the starting material for your culture, the people who are either going to make it or break it as you move forward.

If you're looking to create something new, if you're willing to tear down a few rickety walls in order to build up some new ones, you've got to evaluate each and every advisor currently on board and decide if he satisfies the requirements of your evolving culture, or if you're going to need to show him the door.

Right now, you may not be in a position to do anything about the advisors who fail to meet your Red Velvet Rope Rule, but as soon as you are, you'll need to prioritize this culling. In a perfect world, you'd shed them before you begin bringing new people into your organization. In an imperfect world, you need to be shedding your mismatches as you're bringing new hires into the fold if you're going to survive this game.

Why?

Because you need to have a solid foundation to recruit to.

When you don't have a defined and intentional culture for your business, it's like building a house on a foundation of Styrofoam.

During the interview process, you can talk all you want about how great the culture's going to be, and then, when your new and improved recruits come in, they'll discover that the promised culture doesn't exist—not even close. First thing they'll run into is your cadre of mismatches, the enemy of your claims, and they'll immediately feel betrayed. The mismatches will kill the deal each and every time.

It may seem really scary to start from scratch or to get super small before you get big again. But, if you do things right, within a year, that short-term punch of losing your advisors and your numbers will pay off tenfold in the future.

Exercise 5.3: Identify the Mismatch in Your Organization

If you'd like a template that helps you identify the mismatches on your team, to spell out what makes them inappropriate for your culture, and what you might do about them, head on over to **theculturejunky.com/courses**.

The goal of the system, the machine we're about to build, is to elevate the experience for our advisors, the ones who fit our criteria. To be clear, we can't focus on any one individual, but we can expand the culture offerings for all. If an individual is right for us, the net will catch her and lift her up.

Stage III

———

BUILDING THE MACHINE AND TURNING IT ON

6

THE SELECTION MACHINE

A lot of candidates are attracted to my partner and me because of our culture. Our current advisors have brought many new candidates in by sharing our story and offering glowing reviews. (If you have a highly engaged culture full of people excited about what you do, you've got yourself a goldmine for this very reason.) But that doesn't mean that we're not actively out there recruiting people. That's still part of the job; that doesn't go away. But everything that we're doing to actively recruit people is in alignment with our culture, or at least, it should be.

Most organizations have an established recruiting system or hiring process. They're essentially bringing in folks and running them through a series of interviews. How many of them have added a culture-selection component to this process, however, or implemented it, I couldn't say.

Now, I'm not necessarily looking to replace your current process, but it's time to bring some culture considerations to the table. If you tailor the experiences you deliver to your candidates during the selection process and you obey the Red Velvet Rope Rule you created in Chapter 5, then you've got a culture-based process for hiring. New or experienced, the candidates sitting before you are either in alignment, or aren't. You can either impact them, or not. You either bring them into the organization, because you recognize the fit, or pass. It's basically that simple.

To that end, I'm going to show you how to fold your targeted culture into a foolproof system that involves uncovering the necessary traits in a candidate—the ones that will allow for his or her success in your organization that you listed in your Red Velvet Rope Rule. We'll also assess your own efforts, their alignment with what you profess to want, and their cultural appropriateness.

We've got new advisors coming in all the time because we're all about growth. We've got a number of steps we go through when connecting with candidates, assessing them, bringing them into the company, and getting them up to speed as a full member of the community. In fact, the whole recruitment process is intricately designed long before anyone crosses our threshold. It's a machine unto itself. Every team member has a part in it. Each impact point is part of a system.

Don't forget, this culture thing is just like any manufacturing business producing widgets on the assembly line. There's an order and a reason that the parts go into the machine a certain way. Culture is a business, and there's a product—satisfaction and retention. To produce the targeted culture, we need to know what we're feeding in and what we're getting out. That's when the selection machine kicks to life. That's what we're going to cover in this chapter. Are we producing the right widgets with our efforts, namely, the experiences that are going to keep our people motivated and engaged, or are we not? That's when the execution machine takes over. We'll get to that soon enough.

Culture, as I've said a hundred times, is the average of all the experiences you create. Every single experience that makes up the whole needs to be documented and judged for its cultural alignment. If it's out of alignment, fix it. Or, get rid of it. If it's in alignment, we look for any opportunities to go deeper and make it better. Can we create efficiencies to get more and keep more? Can we enhance what already exists in our current process? Those are the questions we mean to address. Those are the efforts we mean to grade.

The system I'm going to share with you may initially serve as a sidecar to what you're already doing, but, once you understand its power, it will eventually become the backbone of your selection process. The goal is to create a seamless operation that produces the right kind of experiences for all involved so that you and your organization grow and thrive.

It's time to shift from intentional planning into operation mode.

The Law of Attraction

I once asked the new members of a leadership team I was hired to work with to list all of the impact points they have with candidates during the recruitment process. They came up with three things: the first interview, the second interview, and the third.

I looked at them as though they were nuts. What seemed obvious to me clearly wasn't obvious to them. This was a wake-up call.

After this eye-opening meeting, I drew a timeline with an arrow at the end of it. At the beginning of this timeline, I made a mark that represented our first contact with a candidate. Each point thereafter represented all of the experiences and impact points that we have with them, well after they join our firm, straight out through infinity.

I did this because I needed a way not just to educate the team I was working with, but also to see if each of our interactions was attracting the right people and/or making our advisors happy and motivated. Or if they were leaving them cold. (Every time I work with another company, I see my own company through a whole new lens.)

During the attraction process (and every step after), we've got to over deliver the wow factor. We've got to paint this beautiful picture of how it's going to be here. (Of course, we've got to deliver and keep that promise, so we can't have anything detracting from that outcome.) Our job is to go deeper, to make it better, even more in alignment.

I wanted a way to track this stuff on a regular basis, so I turned the timeline into a series of grids: one for the attraction process, one for onboarding, and one for retention. (I'm going to focus on the attraction grid in this chapter and the other two in the subsequent chapters.) Every single time we could touch, talk to, market to, or integrate with a candidate would be documented on the proper grid.

Because we needed to continually judge our efforts by each line item on the grid, each touchpoint, I added a scoring component that ranged from -5 to 5.

- A -5 means what we're doing is pulling us away from our target; it's hurting us. This is the stuff that's killing our culture.
- A 5 is reserved for those things that are dead on; they're creating exactly the experience that we intended.
- A 0 means that we're not having any real impact for whatever reason. In other words, we're not doing it at all.

Every line item on that grid became a conversation point with my team. To ensure that we remain in alignment, we regularly go through and grade ourselves on these impact points. If we find something about them lacking or incongruent, we adjust. (We'll talk more about this adjustment process in Chapter 9.)

The grading process may appear somewhat subjective, but that's a good thing. Somebody on the team—and they're all folks with a vested interest who understand the target goals and the vision—might think a line item rates a 0, and another might think it's a 4. What's really important is that a discussion is taking place. That's where the best results come from, that conversation. If we can improve in that area, and that person now sees that as a 1, and this person now sees it as a 5, we've managed to shift the result in the right direction.

Subjectivity is a good thing at this phase, but it can prove difficult in the initial stages of deciding on your target.

Now we ask questions like this: "During the first interview, how are the candidates greeted as they come in? Is that interaction-in-a-bubble creating the experience that we say we want, the very same one that people we mean to hire are going to want? Is the way we're greeting them doing the trick?" We may decide that it's important enough to include on our attraction grid. We're constantly adding line items to keep our actions front and center.

By the way, if we're not greeting people when they come in, then we'd score that a 0. Right there, we'd have ourselves a gap. But if we're doing it in a nonchalant manner, or we just send that candidate up to the floor, then we'd have ourselves a -3. If our culture leader enters the room right away, says, "Hey, come on in. Let me show you around, introduce you to some other advisors before I take you in the conference room," maybe we'd score that a 5, because that's the experience we're after.

Your methods and message have to speak to the very people you mean to include and exclude. (By exclude, I mean those who would be a poor fit.) Every impact point in the recruitment process has to speak to what your culture is about.

Knowing this, you're going to need to evaluate your efforts.

Exercise 6.1: Create Your Own Attraction Grid

Define the target experience you're after in each step

1. List every impact point you currently have with candidates.
2. Brainstorm even more impact points with your team.
3. Download more resources, templates, and samples at **theculturejunky.com/courses**.
4. When judging each impact point, decide if what you're currently doing is pushing toward or flowing away from the target experience you wish to create. Decide if you should cut it, correct it, or go one level deeper.

Step	Target Experience	Impact Points	Target Culture Alignment Score	Cut, Correct or go Deeper?
			-5 -4 -3 -2 -1 0 1 2 3 4 5	
			-5 -4 -3 -2 -1 0 1 2 3 4 5	
			-5 -4 -3 -2 -1 0 1 2 3 4 5	
			-5 -4 -3 -2 -1 0 1 2 3 4 5	
			-5 -4 -3 -2 -1 0 1 2 3 4 5	
			-5 -4 -3 -2 -1 0 1 2 3 4 5	
			-5 -4 -3 -2 -1 0 1 2 3 4 5	
			-5 -4 -3 -2 -1 0 1 2 3 4 5	
			-5 -4 -3 -2 -1 0 1 2 3 4 5	
			-5 -4 -3 -2 -1 0 1 2 3 4 5	
			-5 -4 -3 -2 -1 0 1 2 3 4 5	
			-5 -4 -3 -2 -1 0 1 2 3 4 5	
			-5 -4 -3 -2 -1 0 1 2 3 4 5	
			-5 -4 -3 -2 -1 0 1 2 3 4 5	
			-5 -4 -3 -2 -1 0 1 2 3 4 5	
			-5 -4 -3 -2 -1 0 1 2 3 4 5	
			-5 -4 -3 -2 -1 0 1 2 3 4 5	
			-5 -4 -3 -2 -1 0 1 2 3 4 5	

Going a Little Deeper

The job of grading our efforts never ends. Just the other day, my partner and I opened the attraction grid. For some reason, my eye caught the

LinkedIn message line item. We dug into the wording, examined it this way and that, and then we modified it because it wasn't quite in alignment. We were getting results from the message, but it wasn't sending the right vibe.

After we modified the LinkedIn message, we moved down the grid. We decided to redefine some of the things we were saying and doing in the interview process. For the most part, we'd been scoring ourselves a 4 in most of the related line items, but we wanted to bring the experience up to a 5. I noticed something I could have easily glossed over if my partner and I weren't intent on ferreting opportunities out.

When a candidate leaves an interview, he or she is handed a packet of information. I took a look at this information packet. It looked pretty good, but nonetheless, I had to rate the way we delivered it to them a -3 from a cultural standpoint. The reason being that we simply hand it to them without a word. They go home with the packet, and two days later, they open it up and wonder what the hell the stuff is. I know, because they keep coming back with the very same questions, all of which are covered in that packet.

We brainstormed a fix.

Along with the packet, candidates would also receive an email video from me going through the packet with them, explaining the components and reconnecting them to the interview. That way, when the candidate got home, he or she could take the time to really look at the information and have a much better experience with me. Both of us would reap the benefit. I called that experience a 3.

The only way to make the packet experience better would be to make it entirely digital, have it flip open before them like a book.

Sure enough, as of this writing, candidates now receive something that looks like an eBook accompanied by a video of me taking them through the material page-by-page. At home, they're getting another explanation of what we covered when we were together, not only jogging their memory but also providing them an experience. Sure, they could read a bunch of one-pagers, but if they can flip through a book and watch a video while having this dude narrate it for them, how much better would that be?

Like I said, attraction is not just about the interview. (Sure, we're going to narrow in on the interview in a bit because this is where your culture becomes the main thing.)

Attraction is all of the methods we employ to bring candidates into the fold.

Even now, there are light-years worth of opportunities lying in front of us that we just haven't recognized yet because we haven't gone deep enough in our thought process.

Here's the takeaway: you need to make the right people want you. You need to design and redesign each and every impact point in such a way as to make candidates feel like they're in the perfect spot. Then, you need to constantly check that you're doing the job.

And don't forget that the goal is to make these people want you *while* you're evaluating them.

The Interview Process

For years, it was just me who conducted interviews. My goal was to, of course, assess the traits of the individual to determine the fit, but also to introduce candidates to our culture by telling stories for the most part, my origin story in particular. You've heard the story. If that resonated with them, if that totally floated their boat, it was clear that we had ourselves a shared enthusiasm about our mission and purpose.

My history parallels with most of the candidates who sit before me. It so happens they're looking for the same thing. They're looking to work the way we do.

As I've said before, I always tell people, "Look, we're going to figure out today if we can be in a room together and if we actually enjoy it, and then we'll get into the details. But this is not a compensation conversation. I've got to be able to see you and be excited to help you, and you've got to be able to see me and be excited to be part of this organization first. Then, we'll get to the details."

I used to say, "The devil's in the details." I don't believe that anymore, not when it comes to taking on a candidate. If we start with the details and then figure out that we don't like each other, that's where the devil is: in the relationship.

As the business grew, however, I realized I needed a way to scale this process. Neither my partner nor I could conduct every interview because time wouldn't permit it. I needed to find a way for others to create connection and excitement.

The Leadership Team

We now have a leadership team that evaluates candidates. These people engage with candidates during the selection process. They serve as a cultural committee, of sorts. They understand our Red Velvet Rope Rule, which qualities will allow people to thrive in our culture, and how to gauge them in the potential hire seated before them. In other words, they know precisely what they're shopping for. These team members are charged with digging into the candidate's background to determine the fit, and having them reveal things that they might not want to reveal because they simply want the job. They fact-find for human traits as much as for a history of success. They drill deeper at each interview level. They go further back in time to determine a candidate's value system and true character.

When my partner and I make our decision about taking on someone new, we start with the team assessment. If the candidate is deemed right for the culture, then and only then do we start looking at the hard data. Does the candidate have what it takes to thrive in the industry, can we support him or her on our platform, can we make him or her better and vice versa? Even though I trust my team's assessment, I fact find. Who is this candidate, specific to our criteria—the criteria built at the organizational level?

Two things are going on during the interview process. We're shopping the candidate—is he or she a good "buy" for us or not—and we're selling him or her on our culture.

There's a fine balance between shopping and selling.

When we bring people in, we've got to make sure that we're shopping as hard as we're selling.

The shopping as hard as you're selling thing is what I had to scale. To get where I am now, I needed some kind of tool that would allow each team member to do both things without co-opting my origin story. (You want to sound disingenuous? Try telling someone else's origin story.)

The Culture Manifesto

Some time back, I brought in two new hiring managers. Outside of the story I told them, my origin story, they knew little of the history of the organization. How could they?

I happened to sit in on some interviews they were conducting. From the way they were talking, it was clear that they'd absorbed the experiences of other organizations, and because of this, our message and objective were getting lost.

I'll explain.

In the financial industry, we're traditionally salespeople first and foremost. That's how we make our living. I've got new hiring leaders coming in all the time, and I have to be aware that they're natural sellers, not shoppers. All they want to do is sell—sell the candidate on the organization, get them in, have them sign on the dotted line. That means gauging the person across from them isn't even part of their lexicon. That they may not actually want to "buy" the candidate doesn't really occur to them.

I also had to get these leaders talking about the right stuff. They couldn't lean on the one-size-fits-all speech they'd been raised on. I had to ground them in our vision and in our Red Velvet Rope Rule. I had to teach them how to speak the language of our tribe, to communicate using whale sounds that can only be heard by other whales.

This is why I created the culture manifesto as a way to remind team members and hiring managers what we're culturally all about and what we're after in a candidate. Because the last thing we want to do is hire a culture killer.

The manifesto is a summary of our Red Velvet Rope Rule. It's just one page in length and answers three critical questions: Who are we? What are we about? Who would be a good fit? It outlines the exact traits of those who are going to thrive in our culture, complete with their core values. It's also a summary of the type of relationship we're going to have with the hire. And, from a purpose standpoint, there's a summary of what a hire can expect as a deliverable when they come onboard: we will bend over backwards to create experiences that will keep them motivated, that will drive them to success.

This culture manifesto is a training manual for assembly line workers, including leadership and staff. It allows for consistency of message and continuity in our cultural story. It allows everyone on the team to remain on the same page. It's the perfect cheat sheet. One glance, and you know basically what we're about, what we're all doing there, and what we stand for. This is what attracted you. This is also what's going to attract like-minded people.

When our management team understands our manifesto, they know not just what we're selling but also what we mean to buy.

When the right candidate hears our manifesto, they're going to want in. We sell them on it.

The manifesto is my origin story—with me taken out of the equation—in bullet point form. It buys precious scalability. Other people can now do what I do.

How I Use the Manifesto in Interviews

I'll often point to the manifesto—because we all use this now—and ask a candidate to pick one of the listed traits under the people section. "Look," I'll say, "we really value people who understand this leverage thing. Tell me about a time in your life where you utilized a company's resources, and it worked for you." They should have some story that dramatizes their appreciation of leverage in order for me to check off that box on my sheet.

The other day, for instance, I was interviewing a woman with a year's experience in the industry. I was listening to her story for clues. "Just, tell me where you're at. How'd you get here? What's going on in your world?" As she spoke, I found a few things that I didn't really need to provoke. I got that she'd been thrown to the wolves.

"I've been trained," she said, "and I'm a very independent person, but I feel like I'm just out there. There's nobody to go to for questions. There's really no team behind me."

And so, there's the whole leverage thing right there. She values that stuff. She's not getting that where she is.

I listened for the other qualities in her story. I picked up on the fact that she was enterprising and entrepreneurial. The other qualities I was going to need to uncover with some questions.

Years ago, I latched on to the acronym HELP. This was the best way to remember the core values I need to see during the interview process. In the moment, it's easy to forget what I'm looking for: honorable, enterprising, leverage, and personal responsibility. I had L and E covered, now I needed H and P.

"Tell me about your relationship with your manager," I said. She stopped and thought.

"You know what? It's not like the dude is doing anything wrong. It's just how it is there." And right there I had my personal responsibility, because she wasn't blaming others.

Nothing about this young woman said, "Just let me sell some shit here, and we'll see how long I can last so I can make a few bucks." Not that you're going to hear anyone actually come out and say stuff like that. You can only pick up on that mindset by actively listening. And what I'm listening for are the very same things I listed in Chapter 3. What do you hear people who value this say? What do you not hear them say?

Exercise 6.3: Create Your Culture Manifesto

1. Describe your four top core values, the qualities you require in a candidate, the ones that make up your Red Velvet Rope Rule.
2. Can you create an acronym to help you remember them?

3. Briefly describe the relationship you intend to have with your advisors.

4. Briefly describe the deliverables they can expect.

Download more resources, templates, and samples at **theculture-junky.com/courses**.

Final Selection Sheet

My leadership team and I spend most of our time focusing on the intangibles listed in the manifesto. Everybody's got to engage with the sheet and make some notes.

If it's all green lights for them, and I'm green lighting the choice as well, it's a pretty short meeting. If some of the team have reservations, if they're not seeing all of the important qualities, it's not a hard no, but we definitely have a deeper conversation with that candidate. We take a deeper look. It might be a no; it might be a yes. We all have to decide if we're willing to take the chance or not.

1. There's another sheet we all work from, which we call our final selection sheet. Along with the standard industry require-ments we have to assess, it, too, has an area for the four traits we value in which we can put notes. Every member of the team has to chime in on those. This prevents anyone from hiring based on his or her gut or mood. This allows us to be system-atic. To download our sample final selection template, go to **theculturejunky.com/courses**.

The Icing on the Cake

I don't have a cheat sheet for this yet, but I should. Before I hire anyone, I've got to be convinced of their fun factor. If we're not laughing in that meeting, I'm out. I'm going to check that no-way box. I may have to battle it out in one of our leadership meetings with everybody else. I may have to give the candidate a second look in case he was having a bad day. But if I'm not satisfied, I'm not taking the candidate on. Because when I see that new advisor on my calendar for a coaching session, I need to think, *Sweet, this is awesome*. I refuse to think, *Oh no. Please not him*.

To be clear, there are certain factors that aren't necessary for success at the firm level. They may be more of a personal preference depending on the hiring leader. Most of us have a "gotta have 'em" status when it comes to a candidate's personality. We might as well establish that fact right now.

Does this mean I need everyone to be a carbon copy of my partner or me? Do I only hire potential beer-drinking buddies? No. I'm talking about people who have a sense of humor that meshes with the organization, who know how to play around and work hard—someone pleasant to be around.

My partner and I happen to be very different people. I'm a front man and an idea guy, and I don't get into the weeds. I'm terrible in the weeds. I'm not a detailed person at all. I can't even manage my own calendar. Jon Rotter, he's pure detail. He remembers everything. He's a personality-driven guy, and he's very detail-oriented. He's a golfer. I'm an outdoorsman. We have very different skill sets, and people engage with us in very different ways

But he's personality plus, no question. We're always joking around and talking. We so enjoy hanging with each other even though we couldn't be more different on paper.

We've been partners for eighteen years, and we've never had a disagreement, let alone an argument. We both like to make money. We both want to have success. We both want to work hard. We both like to have fun doing it. It's mandatory for us that we're laughing every day and enjoying this thing, or what's the point?

And the people we take on? They can be as different from us as night and day, provided they share our core values. But if we don't enjoy being around each other, that's the end of the show.

At the end of the day, if you're not getting the right people, the folks who are going to thrive, then all of your attraction won't mean shit. It's not going to work, because you've brought in the wrong people. From a performance standpoint, they'll fail, and so will you. And who'll be laughing then?

7

THE ONBOARDING
PIVOT POINT

Welcome to the onboarding process. This is the second part of our culture-driven system where we make new hires think, *Wow! This place is even better than I thought.* This is the point they realize they've found their true home. The advisor has signed; perhaps they've begun to transition their business over. Now it's time to make that individual a full team member. It's time to get to know their wants and needs, coach them, and offer up the appropriate resources so you can leverage each other.

This is where we switch gears, moving our attention from the selection machine and focusing on the execution machine. The onboarding process is the pivot point in the system. Now we're building experiences designed to keep our advisors happy. That's the widget we're producing.

The onboarding process, like the attraction process, is systematized. The system is designed to over deliver on the expectation, on the promises you made to the candidate during the attraction process. The system requires you to continually search for new ways to go above and beyond the call of duty, because if a new hire isn't saying, "Holy shit!" then you've got to improve your efforts. You know she's a good fit by now, so it's time to solely place the focus on you and your efforts. The associated experiences you create need to be so special that the new hire remains attracted to you over the course of her career. Are we doing this stuff well? Are we making the effort? Are we doing what it takes to wow them? Those are the questions you'll need to regularly be asking yourself.

The part of the system I'll be sharing with you now spells out a very clear process that will allow you to bring people into the fold, to create a training and mentoring program that fits precisely with the requirements of your culture as well as the needs of your new hire. This is a very defined process that you'll go through with your team leaders when analyzing the roles they'll be taking and the ways they can consistently listen for and deliver on even better client experiences.

Just as I did for the attraction process, I'm going to identify the target experience and list all the impact points in the onboarding process. Again, we're talking about how we systematize these pieces of the manufacturing process so you can deliver a consistent targeted experience. And, we'll talk about evaluating these pieces on a regular basis, scoring each impact point to make sure you're creating the proper widgets.

It's the Things You Don't Think About

The onboarding process is so much more than just training, as you can see from the grid. I'll get to our culture-driven training in a minute, but before I do that, let me emphasize something vital here:

Small things are the big things when creating culture.

Recently, during one of our regular self-grading exercises I do with my team, I found myself staring at the business card line item on the onboarding grid. Something was irritating me, and I wasn't sure why.

I got my first business card when I was twenty-two. New to this industry, I marveled at it, held it up this way and then that way, because it felt like such a big deal. I was shocked that someone would even give me a job that didn't include construction boots and a hammer, let alone a stack of cards. After so many years, I'd all but forgotten the thrill of that early experience.

It occurred to me to question the group. "What are we doing with business cards?"

You know what the answer was?

"Oh. We're good. We put the box of cards on their desk."

That's a -5 experience if you ask me. At best it's a 0. We're not creating any memorable experience by throwing a box of cards on a stupid desk. It was totally out of alignment for us. I looked around and shook my head. This may not sound like a big deal to some, but remember, we measure every single experience, every single impact point that we have with our advisors, down to the tiniest, little things.

I asked the team why we were doing what we were doing.

Seasoned vets, they admitted to having forgotten the thrill, too.

The next day, I went out and ordered these little inexpensive card wallets. I wrote out a standard operating procedure to follow. When the business cards come in, the kit is assembled with the wallet. Then it goes on my desk. Next, a calendar event is dropped into my calendar for me to execute on this experience. I then track down that person, present him with that wallet, and say, "Look what I found." When he opens it, he'll discover his business card. I'm going to talk to him about it, congratulate him, and create something of an event.

What we did with that wallet, with that mini celebration, was to create an experience that was in line with our culture. It's a big deal when people get their new business cards. It behooves us to treat it as such. It's one more opportunity to make someone feel like part of the team—a success in their own right.

And that's the type of stuff that people in my industry simply aren't paying attention to, including me.

Mind you, I'd never have asked that question had I not looked at that grid line item and thought about why the business card was listed there. What is our business card process? What do we do with that? Does it deserve the grade we gave it last time, or not?

Notice something important: we didn't simply throw a dart at the problem with a fix. We backed it up with a three-step process.

Step 1: We identified the gap. The experience we were creating with new business cards sucked.

Step 2: We came up with the solution. We bought little business card wallets and committed two minutes of my time to hand deliver them and make it a big deal.

Step 3: We systematized the process, which is critical. Each step of the process is owned, and our VP of Culture & Engagement accounts for each step.

Exercise 7.1: Create Your Own Onboarding Grid

1. Designate a target experience to each step in your process.
2. List every impact point you currently have with candidates.
3. Brainstorm even more impact points with your team.
4. Identify the motivators present in each impact point.
5. Download more resources, templates, and samples at **theculturejunky.com/courses**.

6. When judging each touchpoint, decide if what you're currently doing is pushing toward or flowing away from the culture you mean to create. Decide if you should cut it, correct it, or go one level deeper.

Culture-Driven Training

I'm going to turn to another line item on the grid, because this is what I get asked about all the time. My peers have their own training process, but they want to know what I'm doing differently and how I integrate culture.

Traditionally, organizations tend to view training as a necessary means to disseminate content or to check off some requirement. For this reason, many organizations place content in some learning platform without a path for advancement or a clear purpose. You can develop a thousand courses, but if your advisor doesn't understand why they matter, your archives will only gather dust.

Here's the thing: if you simply hand a new advisor a manual, or a password to the learning platform, or a one-size-fits-all plan once she's signed the contract, you're all but dropping her into the abyss. That poor person doesn't know why she's doing anything. She's defeated before she even gets going. She could get *that* experience at just about every other shop out there in the industry. Your place—it ain't special.

As a serious point of difference, we provide our new hires individualized resources—resources based on the needs of that person and her business.

We're all about first figuring out who she is and what's going to make her happy and stick around. We pick up some of this in the attraction process for sure, but it's the in-person training, the mentoring that we do, that allows us to better understand the advisor, her why, and her leveragability.

And it's this customized Onboarding Checklist on the onboarding grid that we pick apart—just as we do the other line items—in search of ways to improve on the advisor experience.

Once we know a new advisor's "why," we sit with her and create a plan, the same way that she will for her clients. This plan is based on the numbers she needs and wants to hit. Sure, as part of that plan, there's standardized training involved—which, you'll notice, is also a separate line item on the grid and is, by the way, no better or worse than the standardized training out there—because that's governed by the industry. But where we deviate from the norm is by accounting for her why, what she's motivated by, and keying that into the plan, as well.

Now, let me be clear here: I'm not looking to replace the traditional business plan; I'm looking to get involved in the business plan to ensure success and buy-in.

That motivation stuff is the sidecar that gets tacked on to the training, but that sidecar is what changes everything.

We continually focus on an individual's big "why"—why she's doing this to begin with—to establish that in her own head. In other words, we don't just throw down some numbers she's got to hit; we link them back to her internal motivation.

Remember, from the get-go, we promise to cast a wide web of motivation that creates excitement and opportunities in various ways for all to strive. We beat this drum with our manifesto during the interview process. Our culture is all about providing experiences that motivate the hell out of our advisors.

Let me speak to a nuance for a moment. We have separate strategies for onboarding and retention.

I'll say it again: when we first bring somebody in as an advisor, that experience has got to be really special, because the onboarding process is so sensitive. There are so many things that are going on in that person's head regarding risk and worrying over having made the right choice. Nobody is 100 percent sure. We've got to be so attentive to all of those fears. Unlike during the retention phase, we might not be able to motivate that person at this point, but we can sure deliver on our promises. We can meet their expectations. If we do that, she'll give us the opportunity to shift gears and get her moving in the right direction. She'll trust us when we're helping her put together her plan. She'll begin to teach us how to best motivate her.

Owning the Numbers

The 'old guard' did the math once and came up with the sustainable numbers of activity to get a business like this off the ground and running. What the industry did is take that data, which is good data, and fling it at new advisors, saying, "You just have to do this, and you'll be fine." I was taught that way, and I've got to tell you, I never really understood the "why" behind anything I was told to do. Nobody ever taught me the meaning behind these numbers or how they were key to creating a sustainable practice and getting what I wanted.

I'm not refuting the math; what I'm saying is that the new advisor has to come up with the math on her own. She needs to discover the X + Y= Z of her actions. If she's anything like me, she won't blankly accept a set of formulas simply because "that's how it's done in the industry."

And we've already established that she's like me, like my partner. We hired her because she possesses the enterprising trait. She doesn't need or want a boss, because she *is* the boss. She came on board with us pre-cisely because we promised this kind of relationship.

She creates her own assignments; we participate as hired guns to the business as coaches and resources. But it's hers from beginning to end—the numbers, the goals, the everything.

Advisors begin to own the numbers tied to actions when they con-sider where they want to be in, say, two years, when we can identify the "why" behind that destination during these initial in-person training sessions and really build that up. Then, we can reverse engineer. Nine out of ten times, we come up with very similar math for them to get to where they want to go, but it's their math, not "the industry's." Again, it's not my plan; it's their plan. Then the buy-in is through the roof.

Back to that Choose Your Own Adventure Book from the 1980s. Coming up with your own math—math that I can support as the owner—is a lot like that.

You want to make $75,000 a year? Well, that's above my margin. I can support you. That's cool. I'm not going to force you to make $500,000. Maybe you'll be fine there. But if you wake up two years from now and think, *Shit, I've got to double this thing. Okay, let's go.* I'll get in the passenger seat with you. You're going to drive. I'm going to work the GPS and find the shortcuts for you. Because I'm here to help you, oh entrepreneur, not tell you what to do.

Again, that very relationship is built into our culture.

To really drive home the numbers, the destination, and all that's involved, I help individuals connect to the feeling during our in-person training sessions. What does it feel like when you get there, to that des-tination, to that income level? What does it look like? Where do you live? How do you spend your time? How does that impact your life?

When they see and feel that stuff, they own their plan.

Now you've got yourself a different beast. Now you've got yourself someone who will move heaven and earth to capture that experience.

My job is to generate feelings of purpose and personal growth for my advisors. Going back to our philosophy, the company is built on the cornerstone of partnership—a partnership in each advisor's business. I really want to dig deep and ask a given question in five different ways. It's always about going back to the "why." "Why can you not fail this time? What is the real result of this achievement, and why is it important to you?" It's not my goal, but when an advisor talks about what's driving them, I can't help but appreciate it.

If I can get down to the goods there and really uncover the biggest motivator in their lives, then we can paint the vision that will pull them forward, particularly when things get tough. What will it really look like in twelve or even twenty-four months, or whatever their time horizon is?

"You can go anywhere you want," I tell them. "I've got all the templates and trainings. Use what you want. Let me introduce this stuff to you."

Any training she needs is directly connected to that goal, to the destination she wants to reach. She's engaged in this training because it's hers. She'll eat it with a knife and fork, because she knows that she needs it to get to her planned target at the end of the quarter. It's not about what the firm thinks she should know—check the box on Friday training—it's got a real purpose.

> **Your advisors want a path to engagement, the ability to control their own destiny, with the opportunity to learn every day in a place where their efforts might just change the world.**

Most of the time, I've got other advisors running on the same track. I can see what will work and what will crop up as an obstacle, so it's easy enough for me to point that stuff out and to confirm that what they've put together will work. I can then provide the proper motivation to keep them moving along, but the rest is on the advisor.

Maybe it sounds like a lot of work to come up with an individualized plan to key into someone's big "why," their motivational style. That means, after a while, you'll notice the similarities to five or even ten other advisors and borrow from the plans that work for them. As the owner, I've already developed the resources, the systems, and the know-how to support this type of person's big "why."

Keeping in the Right Lane

Our goals as an organization are all about creating a sustainable business and putting systems in place to serve that end so we don't have to think about it. Our big "why" is because we want to surround ourselves with entrepreneurs who thrive and have fun at the same time and who stick around for years on end. That's the very stuff a candidate keys into during the attraction process that our manifesto drives home. Every touchpoint during the onboarding process, including this in-person training protocol, drives that cultural message home.

My job, our job, is to help accelerate an advisor's business and to create and build the resources to support it. "Here's the menu of resources I've got. What do you need for this first go around? If I don't have it, I'll build it for you." Then, it's a matter of executing the plan. Can we systematize it somehow, do it in a mindless way so we don't have to think about it, which invariably leads to putting it off?

We then pay attention to the little wins of the advisor so the whole coaching or leadership team can celebrate them. If I'm meeting weekly with an advisor, I want to know that she worked the five out of five action items required to move the business forward. Those wins, I'm telling you, are sweet. Do that two weeks in a row, and I'm crowing about the fact that she just strung two wins together.

Coaching your advisors, providing them resources, is a wonderful way to create experiences that will keep them highly motivated. Focus on that in-person training line item, and your advisors will want to learn everything they can about the company and the industry, because they'll see how it can make them money.

By continually gauging how you're doing to that end, constantly revisiting those things that you're doing to make them feel like they're performing and successful, you will buy your advisors' loyalty. The next thing you know, you've bought yourself another lifer. But remember this:

Loyalty is a very hard thing to get, but a very easy thing to lose.

Once you earn your advisor's loyalty, it's easy to feel like you've got it. That's when you let your guard down. The truth is, you have to fight year in and year out to keep it. Which is why we're going to go deeper into the retention process and motivational styles. I'm going to share with you how I systematize experiences that win the hearts and minds of our advisors for years to come.

Chapter 8

MOTIVATION-FUELED RETENTION

We're going to dive deeper so you understand why motivation is key to the system and why it's the very fuel of retention.

Motivation, if you're looking for a definition, is the force that draws you toward something. It can come from a desire or a curiosity deep within you or from an external force urging you on.

Motivation styles, on the other hand, vary from person to person and for different situations and topics. We draw on them all the time, especially when we try to learn something challenging. If you can recognize someone's predominant motivational style—what they tend to be motivated by—you can identify the situations that best satisfy his or her needs.

A motivator is something that provides a reason or stimulus to do something. I'll use this word interchangeably with motivation style if only to make life easier.

A culture is created around motivation, bringing in the right people who are going to thrive in your chosen environment, who are naturally going to want what you've got. What keeps this type of person motivated? That's a question of motivational style. That's the question we owners have always got to be asking ourselves. Which motivator will this kind of person respond to, and which will he ignore? Which motivator will make this other kind of person hungry? Remember, not everyone in your organization will share the same motivational style. Knowing that is precisely how a powerful, engaging culture is born; acting on that information is what buys client loyalty for years, if not for life.

The thing is, juiced-up, motivated people make money for everyone involved, and they stick around, rave about you, and share in your story. That's why culture matters. That's why building a strategic, motivation-driven culture isn't a nice-to-have—it's a necessity.

I learned to create experiences to keep my advisors happy, to keep them motivated, and to ensure stickiness because, as we're all painfully aware, they can pick up and go tomorrow. If they go tomorrow, I don't just lose someone I love to hang out with. I'm out of a lot of money; I'm on my way back to square one.

While we're known for our creativity, for focusing on the tiniest things that others miss, we'll often create experiences like others do through group outings and events, sporting activities, happy hour, and so on. And yet, every experience we create, uncommon or common, is about motivation, understanding who we're trying to influence, the motivation style(s) we're trying to key into, and why. (We'll be spending some time talking about the kinds of experiences you might not think to create in the retention section.) Every question we ask, every survey our people take, every conversation we have—it all comes down to motivation: are we doing it, or aren't we? Are our people happily making the money they want, or not?

I'm a motivation expert because what else do I have? If I'm really going to treat my advisors, the ones I'm going into business with, like the entrepreneurs they are, I can't come in with a stick and say, "Here, I'm taking your business over. Here's how it's going to be." No, I'm all about choosing your own adventure. I'm going to set out a whole bunch of yummy carrots (motivators) for them to chase down.

My deal, my commitment, is to create then release the biggest freaking carrots known to man.

If they see one that they like, let them go chase it down and eat it. I'll build another one.

When I reiterated this philosophy to an advisor I've known for over ten years, he said, "I love chasing down carrots. That's literally why I get up in the morning. I don't have any carrots to chase where I'm at."

I'm like, "Boom, well good. I have a shitload for people just like you. I've got carrots coming up all the time."

Motivation is my job, and you'll want to make it yours.

Getting Good at This Motivation Stuff

Like I said, I'm always looking for ways to motivate individuals. A motivation style was and is something I've paid attention to subconsciously whenever I interact with another human being. I'll have a conversation with a candidate, for instance, and classify him as being recognition-oriented. Something about what he says or does will give me an intuitive hit. Maybe it's something he's shared about his history; I don't know.

I can spot the next person as money-oriented. All he does is talk about how he wants to buy a big house, or maybe he's wearing a Rolex. If the dude is wearing a Rolex, chances are really good he's money-motivated as opposed to recognition-driven. Then again, he could be ego-driven, or even inclusion-driven if he's sees the Rolex as an industry standard. This is an art, not a science.

Intuition is all well and good, but it's hard to teach, systematize, and scale. I'm a measuring guy, a systems guy. I needed something I could work with, something I could teach others on my team to work with, too.

Knowing that everyone is motivated by slightly (or seriously) different things and in different ways, I sat down and Googled the word "motivation." I studied for days.

I broke it down into intrinsic and extrinsic motivations—intrinsic meaning driven from within, for a sense of personal satisfaction; extrinsic meaning driven by external rewards. The extrinsic motivators are the ones you have the most power to directly influence through incentives. (There are tons of great books on this subject, so I won't belabor it here.)

Reading on, I made a list of ten or so motivators that seemed relevant to the financial industry. I then found that I could combine two here, two there, which got me down to the five motivational styles that fit my target culture and Red Velvet Rope Rule qualifiers. People with these five styles would be drawn to who we are and what we offer.

The five motivators include:

1. Recognition
2. Reward
3. Inclusion
4. Money
5. Ego

I should note here that individuals are driven by each of these motivators to one degree or another. One, however, will be primary; others, secondary or tertiary.

You Can Be Crappy at Spotting a Motivational Style

Part of my goal was to try to measure where an advisor "lived" among these five different types of motivation. With practice, you get used to hearing or spotting people's motivational styles, at least that was the case with me, but in the beginning, you won't be very good at it. The trick is to recognize that and to remember the basic motivational styles, continuing to keep an ear and eye open for it.

Even a pro makes mistakes when it comes to pinpointing a motivational style.

For instance, I was working with an advisor three years ago, a woman I thought I'd totally figured out. The way that she talked, everything she did, suggested she was all money-motivated. I have bonuses, I have all these incentives for the strictly money-motivated types (and for those who have money as one of their motivators), which would have been just the thing to keep her excited and going strong.

And yet, while I was sitting with her, she pointed into her office. On her desk sat a trophy she'd won from us. "You know what?" she said. "Nobody's ever given me a trophy; not since I've been in my professional career." She went on to tell me this whole story about how much that trophy meant to her. The look on her face, the way she held her body, astounded me. How I hadn't spotted recognition as her primary motivator, I couldn't tell you. I was wrong.

Thankfully, my net was wide enough, so I still got to her. Thankfully, I don't focus solely on the individual, his or her particular motivation, but on the five styles common to the organization as a whole.

What I'm doing to hit each of those motivational styles is the stuff I sought to track on the grid, particularly in the retention section. That's the stuff I wanted to evaluate with leadership and to systematize.

Casting Your Net Wide

Granted, motivation is unique to each individual, but you don't need to roll out an individualized motivation program for each and every person on your team. You don't have to get an individual's motivation style right from day one. Understanding the major types of motivation, however, focusing on the kinds of things that you can do to spur on different motivational styles, will make your efforts far more effective and more universally applicable.

Cast your net wide, and you can hit multiple motivators with just one practice or event.

Let me give you an example of what I mean by casting the net wide:

We do a summer educational conference halfway through the year. If an advisor qualifies, he can go and bring the whole family. What does an event like this capture in the room? What motivational styles respond to such a carrot? There's recognition. Then there's inclusion. I'm part of the cool club and all that stuff.

With one experience, you can nail three of the five major motivators. Even if you mistook one advisor for being motivated by money, you've likely satisfied his hunger with this event. And you've not just inspired a handful of advisors, but dozens.

Now, during the second half of the year, we host a similar event, usually in some place warm and exotic, that's very easy to qualify for on an individual basis. Yet, we've thrown in a clincher. The individual doesn't go on this excursion unless the entire team meets the goal. In other words, you can't get there on your own.

Suddenly, you've trigged a whole other layer of motivation, styles be damned. Suddenly, that individual—the one who values inclusion or recognition or reward—is all about motivating his buddy sitting next to him because he's made it and really wants to go.

When the team failed to meet the goal, by the way, my people were pissed. I explained that they had to learn to work on their buddies, pull up their own. That's how you create a team environment.

The Retention Grid

It's time to talk about the systemization of experiences for these motivational styles—net casting.

Just as I did for the attraction and onboarding processes, I'm going to list all of the ways I can influence an advisor's experience of our culture during the retention process. Instead of calling these impact points, I'm going to refer to the line items for simplicity's sake as experiences. An experience is something that we regularly host or trigger to deliver a consistent targeted response, one tied to a given motivator (or five). We mean to deliver the experiences our people came to us for in a way that will make them want to stay and thrive.

You'll notice that I use the word experience instead of event. An event, a quarterly happy hour, for example, seems to be what people default to when addressing culture. It's that one thing they believe somehow checks off the box. But the key to this system is bringing to the surface and systematizing the thousand other things we tend to miss because we forget that it's the little stuff when it comes to culture. It's these little things that get totally overlooked.

Remember, every layer in the process is aimed at producing, with precision, the exact product that will ultimately deliver on the target experience that interests them and elevates their engagement.

Of course, we'll be regularly evaluating an experience's effectiveness so we can improve upon our performance or eliminate it altogether. That experience will be graded as being either in full alignment, not happening at all, or totally working against our bull's-eye.

We'll also be confirming that we're hitting the intended motivator with that experience or not and noting it in the associated sidebar.

How we conduct that evaluation, what we do with that information, we'll cover in the next stage of the process. There, we'll also talk about how to go super deep with this stuff and how you can come up with even more creative ideas, which you'll want to track on your retention grid.

Build out your retention grid template by connecting all your current experiences to it. Go super deep with this stuff, and you'll create what I call a monopoly culture—you'll become the only game in town.

Exercise 8.1:
Create Your Own Retention Grid

Define the target experience you are after for each step.

1. List every experience you currently use to connect with your people.
2. Brainstorm even more experiences with your team.
3. Download more resources, templates, and samples at **theculturejunky.com/courses**.
4. When judging each experience, decide if what you're currently doing is pushing toward or flowing away from the culture you

mean to create. Decide if you should cut it, correct it, or go one level deeper.

5. When judging each experience, decide which motivator(s) it will capture in the net.

Checking In with the Individual

You'll notice on the completed retention grid from the website that we have a section for group feedback. I'd like to pause and tease this out for you.

Yes, we create experiences that support the organizational culture, which is composed of the five types I listed. We look at our people as an average; we measure our efforts against the entire population. But we also regularly check in with our advisors to make sure we're keeping them happy. Am I engaging with my advisors the right way, at the right depth, in the right areas to increase their motivation, their profitability, and their experiences?

Again, these are variations on the very same question you'll need to be asking yourself all the time when building your culture machine. How happy are my people, really?

Engagement surveys are the industry standard for measuring engagement, a.k.a. cultural satisfaction. Over the years, I've looked at a bunch of culture-building books that promoted various engagement surveys (designed for the financial industry and others), but none of them seemed to do the trick. I wanted to find a series of questions that would tell me, "I'm actually doing really well with money motivation, but I suck with these other two types." I wanted a motivational style and an engagement survey combined into one.

Eventually, I came to realize that a formal survey wasn't going to achieve what I was after. I mean, I suppose they're great for a start, but what if you find out that what most people want isn't what you want? (That, by the way, is why we started with the target culture exercise, followed by the Red Velvet Rope Rule before arriving here.)

I finally recognized that I already had a much better way to measure engagement to see which motivational styles I was supporting effectively and which I was not. Our people were already coming right out and telling us what was motivating them. If they weren't volunteering the information to me or my leadership team as we moved through the company by talking to them and listening for certain catchphrases, be they negative or positive, they were revealing the gaps in our efforts through our questionnaire process.

By the way, if you really want to figure out how your actions and efforts are being perceived, then find out what people are saying about you when you leave the room.

You might be quite surprised.

Sure, you'll get a lot of feedback from the various surveys you have your people fill out, but, anonymous or not, those surveys still place us in the room. Leave the room altogether, and you get the solid truth.

Questionnaires and Surveys

Looking to systematize the gathering of data—because that's how I roll—I built out a number of questionnaires, which were very simple to fill out for the advisor.

These questionnaires were designed to elicit feedback that would tell us if we were serving their needs and hitting their motivation styles, although we never came out and actually "talked" motivation styles. They allowed us to keep tabs on how people were faring and whether they were going to stick with us or not. Or, at least, we hoped they would.

The information we gathered from these surveys was then documented on the retention grid. My culture director would evaluate the survey and assign it a score. Is this person happy, struggling, or can she hardly wait to get out of Dodge? From the individual scores, she'd rate the company as a whole and insert the grade in our grid.

But then we constructed a far better set of questions as a direct result of our culture manifesto. We know precisely what kind of relationship we want to have with our advisors and the promises we make to them to that end. It's spelled out, right there in our manifesto. But did our clients feel like we were delivering what we claimed we would? We wanted to know: are they truly feeling the love?

Now surveying our people has real meaning. Now I can see that I'm deluding myself, because the answers to the survey tell me so. If we did all this freaking work, had this perfect target we were aiming for, and, damn, it didn't work, well, I want to know that.

The answers to this survey are a precursor of sorts; they'll tell you what kind of movement you're going to see on your indicator sheets, the ones for income, recruiting, retention, whatever you wanted to focus on in the first place. Run this survey and you don't have to wait a full quarter to see if the needle will move. It'll tell you right away.

The Story Machine that Keeps on Giving

A funny thing happens when we have our folks fill out this survey: We get the data we're looking for, but we also get a serious motivational bonus.

Notice that when I send an advisor this survey, I ask him questions that elicit far more than a yes or no. "What makes you most happy about working with us?"

Maybe you recognize that these aren't your typical multiple-choice questions that get ticked off just to get you off an advisor's back. These questions are designed to get very real information, information on an advisor's motivational style, and the effectiveness of your culture-building efforts.

I'll get some amazing stories out of these questions.

I'm after these stories for a number of reasons. Truth be told, I want to pull on their heartstrings when they write their responses. I want them to feel what's been happening for them in visceral terms and to be completely in touch with it. I want them to talk about those moments and why they came and why it's a fit and why they're succeeding and why it's working for them. That's the stuff they go out and share without even recognizing necessarily that they're doing so. I want them to have these stories at their fingertips when someone out in the world asks them about their experience with our company. Once it's written down, it's that much more likely to trip off the tongue, which does wonders for our recruitment. (Remember how I mentioned teaching advisors to share their version of our origin story out in the world? This is just one of the ways we do that.)

I also want to feel something by reading these stories. I want to know what we've done for that person and that they appreciated our efforts. We should do that for everybody who works with us. It feels really good to know that our efforts have real impact. I'm a human being, and that stuff matters to me.

From a marketer's perspective, I've now got lots of amazing stories that I, too, can slip into the origin story of the company when I'm speaking to candidates. Those stories dramatize an experience they, too, can have in beautiful terms. Those stories are the best inducement to joining our organization . . . period.

What I've done with this survey, besides eliciting valuable data to guide my subsequent efforts, is create a story machine. Our people continually sell themselves on the experience we've created and the culture we've built. They continue to feel, to recognize the investment they've made in the place without somebody saying, "Oh look, you're invested." They sell themselves on us.

If we have to remind them of how much we do for them, we've lost.

Exercise 8.2: Create Your Own Survey

Create your own survey based on your culture manifesto. Create some open-ended questions that spawn stories.

Or download a sample at **theculturejunky.com/courses**.

Now, let's explore how to determine the gap, where we're falling down on the motivation job, so we can create a plan of attack, systematize the plan, and manage it.

Stage IV

ATTACKING THE GAP AND SYSTEMATIZING THE PLAN

9

QUALITY CONTROL

Many organizations go about the whole culture-building thing in a way that can only be described as "spray and pray." Like a shotgun versus a rifle, they tend to go off in every direction while assuming they're aiming at the right target, doing the right thing in the moment. Instead of hitting the target dead on with the bullet, their efforts splatter all over the place. Sometimes they hit the rings by accident, but most of the time they mess up the wall. All in all, their efforts lack precision and have little cohesiveness and flow.

But we've got hard data that tells us if we're hitting the targets we created for our company in the form of the culture grid. We can identify the exact places that need work, so we can get back on track and create the results we're after.

Once a quarter, my partner and I pull out our grid. We study the attraction, onboarding, and retention sections, one by one. The job now—because it's quality control time—is to judge it all, line item by line item, experience by experience, to make sure we're producing the widget that we think we are.

It's all well and good to assume we're doing it, but this is the time to get realistic. We sit down like this each quarter to address the inevitable fact that we're not always going to accomplish what we had in mind when we hosted an event or developed a particular practice or experience. And you're going to want to do this, too.

The Big Picture

"Okay," I say, leaning back to look at the big picture, "here are all the impact points we have, all the granular transactions we have with our people. How have we scored each experience in terms of alignment with our culture?"

Remember, we're clear on our target; we understand what our culture is all about; we know what our people need and want in order to thrive. And the assigned score (from -5 to 5) reflects whether the experience is tracking with our target and the people who will react to the target or not.

We run through the 0s where we're not impacting a thing. We run through the negative scores, which are taking us in the opposite direction of our target. Positive fives put us right on target. The 1s, 2s, 3s, and 4s, say we're headed in the right direction, but there's room for improvement.

"We seem to be doing a decent enough job in several areas. We're hitting the target here and here. Over here, not so much."

Wait, I Thought We Were Doing That?

Usually, one of us will notice where we'd come up with a brilliant idea and completely failed to implement it. "Damn, that's such a good idea! Why are we doing such a bad job with it?"

Right there, we've identified a gap just by going through this process. I found one of these gaps in the onboarding section yesterday.

When somebody joins our firm, I used to write a handwritten letter to the spouse welcoming him or her to the organization. That note, which was mailed to the house, had so much impact.

I immediately called my culture director. "I feel like I haven't done the whole handwritten note thing in a really long time." She agreed that I'd fallen off the wagon, because, at the time I'd established that practice, we didn't have this format to be able to go back and make sure it happened.

We're back on it now because it's now a line item on our sheet. We now have a system for it, which we'll discuss soon enough.

I'm a pro at this stuff, and I've got to tell you, I find so many freaking gaps when I go through this process, which is why I can't emphasize enough the need to have someone own this, right down to the minutest detail. If it's not you, then it's got to be someone who lives it on a daily basis, particularly if you're super busy.

The Motivators

After I get off the line with my culture director, my partner and I practically study the retention section with a magnifying glass because it best demonstrates the satisfaction or lack thereof of our advisors. That's where we note the motivation styles each line item hits.

From their perspective, are we doing it for them, or are we not?

What does the survey reveal about them? What's coming up in their coaching sessions? How are individuals feeling about things?

Are our efforts impactful? Are they taking us in the right direction or dropping the cultural temperature inadvertently? Are we, again, hitting the right motivators?

Ah, the motivators.

After assessing the score of a given experience on the retention grid, we move to the right column and tie in the motivator (there may be many, there may be none) that the experience should be spurring. We're all about casting the net wide, so we consider it a good thing if we can cover a number of motivators with one experience.

Five motivators hit with one experience is the freaking jackpot.

If the experience itself has been given a score of -5, it has no business being in our program. (We put a check mark by it because we're going to come back to it when we're putting together our quarterly plan of action.)

On the other hand, if an experience is very much in alignment with our target culture, scoring a 5, but it doesn't yet have a motivator tied to it, we've got ourselves an opportunity for further improvement. (Yes, you can take a 5 and make it bigger and better.) Are we going to attend to it this quarter? Maybe, maybe not. We'll see where our priorities lie.

Alignment, Forgetfulness, Motivators

Notice that while we're assessing the gaps, we're looking at two spots that represent potential opportunities: the line item experience itself and the motivator(s) attached to it if it's in the retention section.

The grid is going to help you identify the gaps in your culture-building efforts and create plans to attack them, too. It'll show you where you're out of alignment with your target culture. Or where you've failed to implement. The grid will also show you where you're failing to hit a given motivator.

No doubt, you're going to spot a lot of areas that could use some serious improvement.

Establishing Priorities

Mind you, we can't plug every gap we discover over the course of a single quarter because culture-building and engagement is a process. To make life manageable, we go after the 20 percent that will do 80 percent of the work.

What constitutes the 20 percent?

Let me walk you through my analysis process, step-by-step:

1. Where are we seriously getting it wrong?

I'm not running any fancy algorithms. I'm literally adding up the 0s, -5s, and such found on the grid. I'm looking to identify the three most egregious areas.

The obvious errors aside, what you're doing to retract from your culture may not be a bad thing, in and of itself. It might be something everybody's doing to build out culture in the industry. But that thing everyone else is doing may not align with your target. You need to either kill it or make some changes to it to get it back in alignment with the target.

If I only find three -5s (or so), those are my new focus.

If we discover a whole bunch of them, way more than we can take on in any one period of time, we jump to step three and focus on the motivation style we've somehow managed to not just overlook but actively undercut.

If there are no -5s, we move to the -4s, -3s, and so on. Rinse and repeat.

2. Where are we getting mediocre results?

Next, we go back to those 1s and 2s and decide if there's something that we can do to feed these scores in the upcoming quarter. (Right now, we're going to treat 0s the same way.) I've got to be able to think of something to do about it right now, and if I can't, I'll put it on the back burner.

> **If I can do nothing to fix it at the moment, I'll move on to something that I can fix.**

I'm just going to go for the line item that I think is going to make the most difference.

Maybe in an attempt to better hit a particular motivator during the previous quarter, we tried something new only to discover that it went against the grain. (We hit the motivator, but the experience didn't support the target culture.) Maybe this quarter we'll come at it from another angle, or we'll move on to something else, recognizing, again, that not everything we attempt is going to work.

3. Which motivators need balancing?

Once we focus on the negative and low scorers, we take a step back and look at the line items with decent scores. Okay, of all the motivators that we're feeding with those experiences, which are getting the most play? What's giving us the highest scores? We're looking at the retention page here because that's where we go after the motivators we mean to hit with an experience.

Maybe we've been all about the money, which is great for those motivated by money. "You know what? We're almost a little too heavy in this spot, and we're only doing one or two things over here for reward and ego, so I've got to balance that out." That's the kind of thing I'm saying out loud.

Maybe we've done next to nothing for the other four motivators that we focus on. "How much effort is going into each one of these motivational styles? How many times am I hitting it? How am I doing with inclusion and recognition? Let's focus on building out these other two, making them more equal."

We need to rectify that imbalance and create some more experiences that will key into one or more of these motivation styles (particularly if they're also associated with low-scoring line items).

My goal is to put a quarterly plan or project together to increase the identified motivational styles to bring some balance into the system. Then, I can systemize an event or practice that's going to bring more attention to those styles. (We'll be talking about project planning and systemization in the upcoming chapters.)

Maybe I work on only one thing if that's all I can manage, but that's the one thing I'm doing for the next quarter.

A Warning about Blind Spots

Here's something you need to be aware of when evaluating the motivational gaps: most leaders are probably good at motivating those who share their primary motivator. Where they get into trouble is ignoring those who are motivated by things that matter little to *them* simply because they can't imagine being influenced that way.

Remember what we learned in stages one and two: you can grow an organization with people who are different from you but who value the same things. People with different motivators can still have the same essential core values. But that doesn't mean you, who are money-motivated, won't ask, "How can they not want more money?"

Well, because that's not what motivates some of the people drawn to you.

You've got to get over that fact.

In order for them to thrive, you've got to hit their motivation style, not just yours, and you can usually do that by casting you net wide enough to offset any gap.

By going through the cultural grid, examining the motivators that are being triggered by a given experience, a leader is able to broaden this scope, eliminating the natural blind spots.

A Perfect Score Across the Board

Let's assume I'm hitting every possible way of motivating my people. I'm not just hitting their primary motivators; I'm even capturing their secondary motivators—inclusion is very important to me, but I still like money—all the way down.

Maybe I've accomplished everything I've set out to do, nailed the target right on the head, and I can sail off into the sunset.

The thing is, there's always work to be done. The cultural temperature will never stay the same, even if you've got your system dialed in.

Every change you make to the machine has the potential to produce some messed-up widgets.

Defective widgets or not, I'm always up for the challenge. There are lots of fun ways to play this game even better. There's more I can do that will widen the net to capture even more motivation styles within a single system or event. Not only that, I can really hit people in all of their motivation styles, not just the primary and secondary ones. By hitting more motivation styles, I can make up for any mistakes I've made in categorizing a particular advisor. It's a whole lot easier to focus on the machine, not the individual.

I always want to do more. I want more experiences that hit more motivators on an organizational level, more 5s, more cohesion, more flow. I want to know that what I'm doing for my people serves multiple purposes. And, when push comes to shove, there's nothing I love more than hearing my advisors say, "The wow moments never stop." That, in and of itself, is the real end goal. That's what makes me happy. And happiness—that's at the center of my target.

Exercise 9.1: Analyze Your Culture Grids

1. List your top five lowest scorers in order of worst to less so. Are there specific motivators that these impact points or experiences were designed to support?
2. List your 0s. This means you've got essentially nothing in place right now to support this experience or impact point.
3. List your top five 1s or 2s. What motivators are associated with these impact points or experiences?
4. List your top scores, your 4s and 5s. What motivators are these supporting? Where are you doing a bang-up job?
5. Which motivators do you have best covered?
6. Which motivators have you failed to support?

We've got a clear lay of the land; we've identified the gaps. Now, let's make some plans that will allow us to raise the cultural temperature during the upcoming quarter.

10

THE FACTORY
BLUEPRINT

Tons of people have written about the Ritz-Carlton and their awesome culture. The hotel chain is famous for their systematized experience. Everybody in the organization, right down to the janitor, listens to the customer, particularly when he or she is unaware. The employee gathers the information and deposits it in a central communication hub, and from there, an experience is created for the observed guest. Eventually, these experiences become standard operating procedures.

These customers, these guests, talk more about their experience at the hotel than their actual destination. The Taj Mahal could be right out their window, yet they're going on and on about the lemon sorbet that got delivered to their room when they didn't even order it. All because someone on staff overheard them talking about the refreshment they were craving.

I can't help thinking about that when I check the industry forums and social media sites. I'll find post after post that screams, "Hey, look at our culture! Breakfast Fridays!" accompanied by snapshots of three employees scooping scrambled eggs onto a paper plate. There's always some guy in the corner barely containing his boredom by staring at his phone. Most of the time, these underwhelmed breakfast-eaters look like they wish they'd gotten the extra hour of sleep or been allowed to sit at their desks alone. Guaranteed, I'll check back next month and find images of three-legged races in the parking lot. The month after that, chair massages in the conference room.

Those experiences created by The Ritz-Carlton, however, the ones that wow their customers, are planned out right up front. They're all customized, systematized, automated, and intentional. There's nothing random about them or spurred by the latest craze spotted on other hotel sites. They're all about someone having picked up on what the customer craved. That's what we want to do for our customers, our advisors, the folks who make our business work, who talk about us every chance they get: plan automated experiences that make them rave.

I read somewhere that 25 percent of all North American companies have a culture plan. Well, how many of those companies have positive execution? What kind of execution? I'm guessing 5 percent of that total implement their plan properly and then get *any* kind of result, let alone Ritz-Carlton results.

This is why I go crazy listening to owners on their soapbox. "Culture is everything," they say. "Culture trumps strategy, all the time."

My industry got a hold of that mantra a while back, and they couldn't stop saying it. I'm sorry, but that rings hollow, because nothing has changed. You don't have to look further than our unsatisfactory retention rate to know I'm right.

I know intentional culture. And by this point, you do, too. You get that you need to first identify your gaps before you start throwing random events and practices into the mix. Then, on a regular basis, you need to measure these experiences to see if they're effective or not.

The job at hand is to identify the options, to pinpoint experiences designed to delight our advisors, to focus on the one (or two or three) thing(s) you're going to do consistently for this quarter.

And it's not just you, the leader, who's going to do these things. And you're not just going to randomly task these things out. You're going to create a workable plan with well-defined steps and get other team members involved.

This quarterly plan is your factory blueprint. It keeps everyone on the assembly line doing what they're supposed to do, which is creating that targeted experience you can't get anywhere else.

Creating the Plan

Nothing happens without a plan. Like everything else that comes off the back of it, the planning process has to be automated. Just because you want to do good stuff for your people doesn't mean you'll get to it, because you're simply way too busy. (We're going to go further into automating/systematizing experiences in the next chapter.)

Quarterly planning, which you no doubt do already, needs to have a culture-building component attached to it. This is the sidecar you'll want to hitch to your current process.

My business partner and I have gone through the same planning every quarter for the last, I don't know, fifty quarters. We go through the same process in the same cadence. Culture grid in hand, we approach it the same way each and every time so that we make sure we're covering all the bases, that we're judging the right things, and that we're making educated decisions.

We spend those two days out of the office and walk through the following steps:

1. Reviewing the vision we had and have for our culture.

We're twelve years in. Our vision is different today because it's expanded. Is it better than when we first started out? I don't know, but it's more appropriate for where we are now and what we're trying to accomplish. Our culture continues to evolve alongside us and alongside our business plan. We know what we want, we know where the gaps are, and we're all about intentionally doing stuff to bridge those gaps.

2. Then, we look at our culture grid at the very gaps we've recently pinpointed—be they low scores or missed motivators.

What's the one thing we're picking to go after for this next quarter in order to raise the temperature around here and make our people feel even more supported, energized, and valued, so they not only stick around but also brag about the experience to their family and friends? That's the question we ask each other when we sit down to map out our plan, our execution strategy.

3. What do we need to build, how are we going to run the play, what's the expectation, and who will be accountable for implementing the plan until we reconcile at the end of the quarter? Once we answer this series of questions, we record all of these details.

As I've said, we've been doing this forever. We manipulate and move and change and recalibrate. For those two days, we get to be the boss. We get to make all of the decisions and all of the plans, not just for us, but also for everybody on our team.

The thing is, during the other twenty-eight or so days of the month, our job is to be the best employee. We simply plug ourselves into the plan, come to work, and just implement. Neither of us makes any changes along the way. If we have new ideas, they go into a vault. We save the ideas and make sure that when we come back around and do reconciliation, we give them a good, hard look. That's when we can make the rules again.

I start to look at some of those "brilliant" ideas I came up with while I was in implementation mode, and I'll be like, *that's the dumbest thing ever. I can't believe I actually wrote it down.* But at the time, I would've traded everything to do just that because I was in the crunch silo of my day, not looking at the grand scope, the bigger picture.

Stick. With. The. Rules.

You have to set this sucker free and become your best employee from an implementation standpoint. You don't get to make the rules anymore when you're in employee mode. We don't revisit any of our decisions until we sit across from each other during our planning session for the next quarter. Neither of us makes any changes until we're back in the boss chair, and then we go right back to being the best employees on the planet. Boom. I've got my seat on the bus, and I just go to work. I fall into the familiar cadence. No second-guessing, just working the plan long enough to see if our changes move the needle in the right direction.

As the owner, you'll need to wear two hats.

You're the planner in a Stetson, and then you're the implementer in a ball cap.

Most people spend all their time second-guessing their plan because they think they're still in boss mode and they can negotiate that kind of thing away. If you want to cut the bull and the perseverating and just make a decision and act on it, this is how you do it. You wait long enough to see how it turns out. You trust your planning ritual, your process.

At the end of the quarter, look at the data. If you don't see the uptick you're after, try again in a different way. There's no need to beat yourself up. "Okay, I came up with this; this was the best shot, the thing that I thought would make the biggest difference, and I implemented. Did it do it? Maybe, maybe not. So, what's next? Who's next?" And then, you move on.

During the initial planning stages when you're getting clear on your business, the outcomes that you're after, and the culture you're looking to create to serve that end as well as draw the kind of people to you who are going to make you happy, there's little room for subjectivity or for experimentation. Because we can't have a fuzzy target, right? That's why we've got to get as granular and as detailed as possible to hone in on that target and bring it into sharp focus. But when we get into this quarterly planning phase, we're making assumptions, judging the items on the culture grid, and judging the things that we're currently doing. Subjectivity and experimentation are okay here, because that's the stuff that's going to spawn creativity. Don't be so afraid of getting it wrong or of failing to get a result you're after. Relax. Make your best guess, work the plan, and wait long enough for the results.

Think in Terms of Quarters

We do everything on the quarter.

What's a quarter? Twelve weeks? Well, throw a holiday onto the calendar, catch a cold, and you've got ten short weeks to get an outcome.

It's pretty easy to piss away a quarter, so if you have too much stuff you're trying to jam in there, nothing gets done. That's why it's essential you limit your focus to just one or two projects so you can nail them. Next quarter, you can turn your attention to something else.

Before we systematized our approach, we wouldn't give things enough of a chance to work. If we didn't get any results within a week, I'd say, "Screw it, there's probably something wrong with our approach." It often takes an entire quarter, if we build a project right, to see some sort of traction or make something dramatically better.

Also, if the target continually shifts based on mood, there's zero chance that our culture-building efforts are going to get the results that we're after.

If you can keep your target solid, at least for a quarter, independent of mood and all the crap you see on your social media feed, you've got a shot at effecting real outcome.

Planning with a Blank Culture Grid

If you're going through this planning process for the very first time, you're looking at a lot of blank space on your culture grid. It's time to put some experiences in there.

You're probably doing something to make your people feel part of the fold already, even if it's Breakfast Friday. Don't stop doing what you're doing, because you're here for a reason, and things are working to some extent. Otherwise, you wouldn't have picked up this book. Your instincts are good enough that you'll discard the stuff you don't need to be doing and bring in the stuff that works. Over time, you'll just evolve.

If you're a scratch office, okay, great; what do you want to do? What are some ideas you've got rolling around in your head? Let's get something in here, spin it for a quarter, and then judge it and figure out where you want to go next.

All random acts of breakfast aside, what event or practice could you experiment with this quarter to inspire your people to make them feel warm and cozy?

How will you know if your experiment has been successful? (We're going to really dive into this in Chapter 12.)

What steps will you (or your team members) need to take in order to implement this new thing you're going to try?

Who's going to be responsible for what and when?

These are the questions you'll need to be asking yourself when you sit down and plan. If you've got a team in place, allow them to further refine your ideas when you present your ideas.

Through experience and a willingness to experiment, we've become pretty good at coming up with creative approaches to get what we're after in our culture.

I'll give you some options for raising the temperature that have worked in the past for us and what we've done to bridge the gap, many of which you'll be able to implement in your organization. I'll start with low-scoring experiences on the culture grid and then move to the motivators that need better support.

What You Could Implement this Quarter

I talked about my working through the analysis process, looking for gaps in the grid, and realizing that, like a fool, I was no longer writing welcome notes to the spouses of new hires. But let me tell you why that experience was on the grid to begin with, just to get you thinking about what it is you're after and how you're going to accomplish it.

Spousal Welcome Notes

Here was the perceived opportunity (or problem, in regular people talk): We were not engaging spouses and significant others until, in many cases, months after hire. We'd missed the chance to create a sense of inclusion for the biggest support system our hire has. When we do this, I'll hear, "Nobody does that! My wife was so touched by that note that you wrote, Jon." Sending those notes is probably one of the most important things we can do because, if we don't have the spouse behind the advisor, they're screwed, and then we're screwed when it comes to their engagement. That spouse will end up saying, "You know what? This is too hard. Go get a real job with a salary. We don't need this garbage."

We also realized that because of our haphazard approach, we had no real control over the timing of these mailings. Sometimes they were posted the day after the spouse was hired, sometimes weeks later, sometimes, not at all because the task had fallen off one of our desks.

The solution seemed simple enough: the CEO would send a handwritten, personalized welcome note to the spouse or significant other when a new advisor joined the firm.

But if you're going to systematize this stuff to ensure that it gets done, you've got to break down a task into the steps involved. (Again, we're going to spend more time talking about systemization in the next chapter, but I'm going here now so you see how detailed you'll eventually want to go when planning.)

We created an SOP (Standard Operating Procedure) around this, complete with clear timing.

1. Trigger—contract completion.
2. Licensing/contracting immediately alerts VP of Culture & Engagement when complete.

3. VP of Culture & Engagement pre-addresses envelope with blank card and delivers to CEO with deadline attached.
4. CEO writes and returns to VP for send out.
5. VP of Culture & Engagement owns this process and is responsible for executing it flawlessly and tracking it to completion.
6. All steps documented.

See how my mind works?

Let me give you another familiar example off the same page of the grid. Let's go back to the business card line item, the ritual we created around their presentation.

Business Cards

Here was the perceived opportunity: by treating the business card delivery as an afterthought, we'd missed the chance to create an inline experience. We were detracting from the experience as it applied to the target culture on our grid, thus the negative score. Instead, we could raise our score by using the cards to talk about the hire's future and the fact that we're proud to have his or her name on the card. And in one fell swoop, we'd also be supporting the ego and inclusion motivators.

The solution, if you remember, was simple: we'd purchase business card wallets and place a few of the new cards in it. Senior leadership would then sit down with the new hire and hand-deliver them, using them to express our excitement and pleasure.

To systematize the process, we broke the task down into steps, creating an SOP around them.

1. Office manager alerts VP of Culture & Engagement that cards arrived.

2. VP preps cards, holder, and box.
3. VP hands to Senior Leadership with deadline.
4. VP owns process and must track to completion.
5. All steps documented.

Now, remember, we're looking to raise our grid line-item scores, but we're also looking to focus on certain motivators we may have given less attention to during the past quarter, even if we're not noting them on the attraction and onboarding pages of the grid. Here's something we came up with when looking for ways to boost a motivator.

'Atta-Videos'

Here was the perceived opportunity: we wanted to celebrate certain advisors who'd hit a milestone or done something noteworthy. We also wanted a way to not just support the recognition motivator, which we'd done a pretty good job with, but to also increase inclusion and go even deeper with it. Like the welcome letter we sent home to the spouse, we wanted something to draw in those closest to our advisors, the people who influenced them at home. We wanted our celebrated advisor to be talking about the responses he got from those at home for days because he felt super proud.

The solution went as follows: the CEO or president would replace the traditional "Atta-boy/girl" note we sent an advisor for a job well done with a personalized short video.

The steps were simple: once the CEO recorded the video, he would text it to the person being acknowledged via the company system. (These videos live in their text files and make it easy to share with people at home.)

The other day, I had a guy tell me that he'd showed his wife the video when he got home. I'm like, *Boom, nailed it.*

By the way, it would have never occurred to me to do such a thing had I not had that grid in front of me, had I not stepped back and looked at everything I was doing from a distance, separate and apart from all the noise. And that's why this culture thing we've created is a forever deal for people.

What more could we do to nail inclusion? That's what we asked ourselves right then. What other practice could we come up with that would serve that end?

$2 Birthdays

Here was the perceived opportunity: we wanted to increase family inclusion with our advisors so that everybody felt part of the team.

The solution was as follows: each year, every advisor's child under the age of twelve receives a birthday card from leadership with a message and a $2 bill within.

The steps were simple:

1. During contracting and licensing, the office manager has the advisor complete the personnel/business continuity sheet that captures each kid's name and D.O.B.
2. VP Culture & Engagement is responsible for keeping ample $2 bills on hand.
3. Monthly birthday cards are prepped one month in advance and given to senior leadership for inclusion of message and signature. Deadline included.
4. The cards are returned to VP and distributed accordingly.
5. VP of Culture & Engagement is responsible for flawless execution.

Believe me when I tell you that the card and $2 bill went a long way in the creation of wow.

Motivator Options

Because we're all in the motivation business, let's talk about all the ways you can support your people's different motivational styles. Chances are good that many of the common motivators you'll need to support are the same as ours.

If you're new to this culture stuff, you may not feel particularly creative. Sure, you understand that you may be hitting it for certain motivational types in your organization and failing miserably with others. But what kinds of things can you do to up your game for all involved?

The following are motivator scenarios that will give you some great ideas. Pick one, tweak it, then implement it during the next quarter. And just a quick caveat: what you do by way of implementation will differ based on your resources. Don't bite off more than you can chew, because you'll wind up walking backwards in the end.

What to Do for Those Motivated by Recognition:

We've already talked about Atta-videos and how they boost recognition (as well as inclusion). But let me tell you about another practice we put into place to support this motivator.

Barbara, who's been part of the culture for many years, was crushing it to make an incentive involving this sporting event, watching the Chicago Cubs play from right behind home plate. I approached her one day and said, "I never knew you were that big of a Cubs fan." She laughed and explained that she simply loved winning.

Now, Barbara makes plenty of money. She could buy tickets behind home plate anytime she wanted. But that's not what motivates her. Sure, she likes to win, but she was doing what she was doing for the inclusion. More, she likes the recognition, though she would never admit that.

There's a whole bunch of ways you can see if your events are motivating people the way you planned. Barbara, for one, loves to see her name up on the flat-screen monitors we've got in the back where we all sit. That's when I really understood that she was motivated by recognition. Those monitors are big, placed up high so everyone can see them, and they rotate nonstop. Splashed across the screen are reports of all the good stuff people have accomplished, where people are in the rankings, who qualified for one incentive or another, a congratulations to this person and to that person—basically a scorecard of the carrots.

Everybody watches those screens so they can see their name and their picture up there with those of their peers. Those motivated by recognition, Barbara included, eat that up. How do I know? Because things got better when we put those monitors in. (Again, we'll talk about how to measure the effectiveness of an event in Chapter 13.)

Here are some other arenas and ideas that boost the recognition motivator:

RECOGNITION:

- Social media
- In-office signage/monitors
- Newsletters
- Handwritten notes
- Atta-Videos
- Trophies/plaques

What to Do for Those Who Are Motivated by Rewards:

We've got a club recognition program that ticks the reward and inclusion motivator as well as recognition. Each qualifier gets a branded golf shirt, similar to those that can be purchased through our marketing department, except there's a special patch on the arm signifying their club qualification and the year they achieved it.

You'd be absolutely amazed how proud our folks are to display these shirts. They're positively on fire when they can collect them year after year.

Want some more ideas?

REWARDS:

- Social events
- Marketing expense
- Education reimbursement
- Trips
- Private office
- Logo apparel

What to Do for Those Motivated by Ego:

Like Barbara, many of our advisors just like to win. That's what drives their performance. To that end, most of our quarterly incentives include an extra layer of fun or gamification. Gamification ensures that there's a winner.

We do a "summer madness" that mirrors the NCAA March Madness tournament. Everyone in the firm is randomly placed in brackets. Then, they square off against each other and, following a specific set of rules, score points.

The winner gets his or her name engraved on the Traveling Trophy and receives a prize. So, we manage to tick off recognition, reward, and inclusion as well. (I'll tell you more about this in Chapter 12.)

Here are a few more suggestions to get you thinking:

EGO:

- Let them lead. Leadership doesn't just mean management. Allow them to teach a class, mentor, or speak to the group.
- Include them in decisions. Run potential changes or ideas by them and value their opinion.
- Acknowledge their strengths. Talk about their strength in front of others. Tell them about the stuff they have that most others don't.
- Create opportunities for them to win. It doesn't need to be a big blown-out contest, but a small challenge between two people is more than adequate.

You've seen plenty of examples and should have a handle on the direction you want to go. It's time you decide on your top priority and create your quarterly plan of attack.

Exercise 10.1:
Create Your Quarterly Plan of Attack

1. Build your quarterly plan/factory blueprint.
2. Identify detailed experiences to focus on.
3. Assign roles/duties to your assembly line workers.
4. Download more resources, templates and examples at **theculturejunky.com/courses**.

11

THE ASSEMBLY LINE

No matter which experience we pick to implement in a given quarter, the only thing my partner and I are thinking about is our ability to create the assembly line, the systematization that will produce the desired result. A system allows us to consistently push out a product—namely a cultural experience—as fast as you turn the belt. These customized practices and events are part of the machine, one with multiple assembly lines and multiple line workers involved.

The longer that belt is churning out the intentional experience, the more the culture starts to shift or develop or evolve to meet the target.

Remember: nothing's going to happen overnight. Like a workout regimen, nothing of substance happens if you simply follow a course of action for six hours or days. Work the program for twenty minutes a day for two years, and you've got yourself a different result.

I'm a huge fan of automating because I hate having to think. Because when I think, I get into trouble.

Here's something I hear a lot: "Well, I meant to do that."

"Well, did you do anything about that?" I'll ask my well-intentioned peer, the sheepish soul who recognizes his own bull as it falls from his mouth.

"No, I wanted to. I just didn't have time. I forgot."

Thing is, what you intend doesn't change the experience for the human being on the other side of the equation. If you automate, those things will happen regardless of what else you've got going on, and your people will feel the impact. The game will change.

I also happen to be a huge fan of not trying to manage these changes alone.

I've turned both the leadership and support team into assembly line workers who together create the widget.

They take the same actions day in and day out, so they don't need me hovering overhead. I tell my people all the time, "Look, you live in this ecosystem, so when you find a better way to do something, get after it, because I'm just going to pop my head in every once in a while to check in. If there are problems, then you have to drag me in, and we'll fix them together. But ultimately, you have full ownership. Bring me the ideas if you can take what's in place right now and improve upon it."

Team Meetings

My team identifies with our advisors the same way I do, so I get them all together in the same weekly meeting, because that's where all the culture stuff comes up. If I want to know if my assembly line is spitting out the right widgets, I ask them and my other leaders. I'll ask them what they think—if what we're currently trying is making a difference. In fact, I'll get out there and conduct my own ad hoc interviews before implementing anything major. I'm all about getting their buy-in.

"Hey, I'm thinking about doing this," I'll say. "What are your thoughts?" I almost try to get any sort of change to be their idea, because, once I press play on the thing, they'll inevitably give me push back. Good or bad, people don't like change. But once they've bought into the change, they're going to run to the top players and sell them on it.

"Oh, yeah, don't worry about it," they'll say. "It's perfect. It's actually great for us because of this and this."

By the way, that's part of systemization. Get the buy-in of the leaders, beyond management, especially when you're considering a change that can be perceived as bad news. When something changes that people get a little bit dicey over, they go there first, not to my partner or me because we're the bosses.

My partner and I have made the decision about which projects we're going to focus on for the quarter. But when we bring our plans to the team meeting, we start with who's going to own a tactic, new process, or event—who's going to be responsible for the various pieces of it. We identify the players for that piece, for that system, and then we discuss the outcome we're looking for. "What are we striving for? What's our win in this thing?"

My partner and I may have come up with a brilliant idea for the quarter and sketched out the dance steps, but we don't always trust our instincts. We've had plans and ideas that we didn't bother systematizing because we could tell they were going to be a failure from the get-go. In fact, we have these brilliant, no-go ideas all the time. I may think our idea is a winner, our plan totally workable, but I trust my people to tell me if they see something that I don't.

Which is why, in the meeting, we go deeper. We ask the attendees:

- Is this thing we want to do possible?
- Do we know what to do?

- Is there something that we have to learn along the way to get this thing to come out the other side in the green?
- Do we understand what happens if we don't do it?
- Is this realistic?
- What else to we need to do to set ourselves up for a win?

Everybody knows his or her place in that room. They know the person who is responsible for an action during our week and for the next update. What do we need? We need to bring some other people into it to take it to the next level? Okay, you got it.

Unlike a lot of bosses who never let go and who keep their hands on all the chess pieces, I let my people own it. Where do I need to be in the mix? Sometimes, I'm just consulted on a project. Sometimes, I'm out of it, and I just react to whatever is brought up in the next meeting. Those weekly meetings allow us all to know precisely what's going on at every point in time anyway, so it's easy to trust the system and the line workers. There's no micromanaging or shirking responsibility on my part. Change won't work any other way.

Systems allow you to delegate, not shirk.

Let me give you an example of how I get my team members to truly own the process.

Two and Two

We have this practice called two and two. My partner and I came up with this idea during one of our planning days when we were trying to come up with a way to support those motivated by inclusion during the retention phase.

Each week, everybody on the team, including my partner and I, must bring to the table two things that they learned about someone in the organization. Now, this thing can't have anything to do with one's regular job or role; it has to be personal. Which means that each of us has to get off our backsides and go talk to people—not about business, but as human beings.

Once we find out something noteworthy, we share it with the team in the next meeting. That way, all nine members get to hear eighteen personal things about our advisors.

The second part of the equation is for each of us to share two things that we did during the previous week to create a unique experience. These experiences, by the way, are typically based on the information we learned about others the week before. In other words, the "twos" feed off each other. We get information, and then we can create an experience around it in the next seven days.

These experiences don't have to be big, grand gestures—although some of them get pretty blown out—in order to satisfy the "rules" and to be entered into a competition, where you can win a pot of money. (Notice how we cast the net wide; bring in those team members motivated by money. And ego.)

Whoever has the best information bite each week gets entered into a pool. (If anybody in our regular weekly meetings fails to gather two pieces of information about someone in the organization, he or she has to pay $20 into the kitty.) We draw one of these names out each quarter, and the winner takes home all the money. Last quarter, one of our marketing people won $350. This, as you can imagine, is highly motivating.

Two weeks ago, my guy Aleks heard in the meeting that our advisor, Rick, was going out of town to see his parents in Arizona. Aleks wrote that down. Later that week, thinking he could create an experience out of the information, Aleks approached Rick and said, "Hey, I hear you're going to see your parents, what's going on?"

Rick's like, "Oh, it's my dad's birthday!" He continued with the story. "I'm just really nervous because my driver's license expires, so I have to remember to bring my passport or I'm not getting on the plane."

Aleks puts a little note in his phone with the travel dates. The morning Rick is due to fly out, Aleks texts him. "Have a great trip. Don't forget your passport."

When Rick came back from his trip, he couldn't stop talking about what Aleks had done. "How the hell did Aleks remember, two weeks later, about my passport and text me in the morning to make sure that I had it?" He answered his own question. "I'll tell you why. Because he cares."

Sure, Aleks cared and had the best of intentions. But, absent a system and our process, it's possible that life could have gotten in the way, and he'd have failed to create that experience for Rick.

Believe me when I tell you our advisors feel seen, because they are. People who feel seen tend to stick around.

P.S. Did you notice how inexpensive this form of motivation is?

Now, let me come back to Two and Two as a systematized event.

When my partner and I thought up this concept during our planning day, we'd become clear on the outcome we were after and the steps that would be involved.

Here was the perceived opportunity: we wanted to learn more about our people so we could create more customized experiences to drive our culture.

The solution we came up with is as follows: every Tuesday during our leadership meeting, each of the attendees would be required to share two new personal things they'd learned about someone in the organization as well as two things they did to create a customized experience for someone.

As with everything we do, we broke the task down into steps, and created an operating procedure around them.

1. Meeting prep sheets have been created and are on hand.
2. It's the first (and most important) thing addressed at the meeting (If done last, it's an afterthought).
3. If someone is not prepared with two and two, they have to pay $20 to the kitty.
4. We vote on who created the greatest experience that week.
5. At the end of each quarter, we put all the names of weekly winners in a hat.
6. Draw one name and give them 50 percent of the pot.
7. My partner and I match the other 50 percent and take the entire group out.
8. This part of the meeting is run by the VP of Culture & Engagement, who is responsible for the gamification aspect.

If you have ten people attending a meeting reporting on two experiences, over the course of fifty weeks, you've created 1,000 intentional customized experiences.

As I've mentioned before, gamification is another powerful motivator. If it's fun, people will participate.

Having Good Intentions is Not the Same as Being Intentional

I'd like to pause long enough to drive this point home.

Everybody on my team, and they're all awesome human beings if I do say so myself, wakes up each day worried about the shit they've got to do, not the stuff that they should do. Sure, they've got the best of intentions. They're going to hit the ground running and spend the day spreading joy and creating success. But then, life gets in the way. And the best-laid plans get tossed to the curb. Which is why all the things that go into creating a culture need to be systematized. Sure, the personalities of those involved, the emotional side of the equation have to be taken into account at every step, particularly during the planning stage, but without systems dialed in, execution will go right out the door.

Systems are what allow for mindless execution. We don't think about whatever it is we planned to do; we just do it.

My calendar, a system in and of itself, tells me what to do. Thanks to all the work we did in the gap-identification and planning sessions, I know why an entry on the calendar is there. I know damn well that these things are in my calendar in a certain way at a certain time so I can hit my goals. They're my brainchildren, these calendar entries. If I don't like them, I can either change my goals or quit bitching and go back to work.

Culture is made up of the little things because little things are the big things.

Which is another reason you need to think in terms of systems. You know what happens when you've got a million little things to do. Something vital always falls off the plate.

Exercise 11.1: Your Calendar

1. Create a calendar of rewards/recognition/incentives.

When we were kids, we always seemed to have something to be

excited about—perhaps a birthday, holiday, or a family vacation. For the most part, these events were spaced out and balanced throughout the year. However, if everything fell in the same month, we'd have a much harder time differentiating and find ourselves overwhelmed. A busy, jam-packed month also created quite the lull in the other eleven months of the year. That's why it's important that our recognition and rewards be balanced out on a timeline, so that each individual motivator can get the attention it needs and the focus to achieve it.

2.   Choose one strategy to systematize. How will you make sure this thing happens? Who will be in charge for what? How will you know if this strategy is working? What will it look like?

Let me give you an example of another little thing, one that's been systematized, because I'm all about giving you more and more ideas to spark your creativity.

The Life-Event Grid

At some point, we recognized a gap in our culture grid. We recognized the need to better motivate those driven by inclusion.

As usual, my partner and I brainstormed ideas that would serve this motivator above and beyond what we were already doing to that end. How could we reach out beyond the advisor and connect with his family? How might we do that? How frequently could we do that? What are the options? How could we systematize them? What could we do for an individual advisor without making others feel as though we're doing more for one individual over another, playing favorites?

What could we use as an excuse to make people feel seen and valued? Birthdays, wedding anniversaries, children's birthdays, graduation days—that's the normal stuff that gets noted.

But what I continually ask myself is, "How can we make this bigger? What are we missing?"

We thought of everything that could possibly happen in somebody's life, because, quite frankly, I don't want to think of that kind of stuff on the fly. We put together a life event grid so we could add to the repository as the ideas came.

One day, after a Tuesday team meeting and the two and two recitation, I found out that the son of one of our advisors was just hell-bent on acing the SAT test. Immediately, I added, "taking the SAT" on the life-event grid. I emailed that kid once I got the address from his mom to wish him luck. He thought my message was the greatest thing to ever happen to him. He responded, "I'm not going to let you down." That interchange brought tears to his mom's eyes. Because not only is she included in the organization, so is her son.

Emailing that kid directly cost me nothing. I didn't buy him. I didn't send him an edible arrangement, but I made the kid's day and gave the mom tears of joy. That felt good—really good.

Exercise 11.2: Create Your Own Life-Event Grid

What will you capture on a regular basis? What information will you need? How can you think even bigger?

Or go to **theculturejunky.com/courses** and download a sample Life Event Grid.

Ripples in the Pond

Again, the only way to affect outcome consistently, to a point where we can measure it and tweak it, is to systematize a practice, tactic, or event. That way, if we can push the needle forward and keep this thing doing what it's supposed to be doing, we'll get to our mark. And then, we can create a new one, and another one after that.

But here's a real issue we have to contend with: everything we do has multiple effects, not unlike throwing a rock in the water and producing a bunch of ripples. One tactic, event, or practice has the capacity to impact everything else, so I need to make dead sure that a change I'm looking to make doesn't disrupt what's already working in the ecosystem.

My partner and I remind ourselves of the ripple effect a lot. We can't stop doing what we're doing just because we have new ideas and new opportunities if those current things work. We're human. We sometimes get a little bit bored by doing the same things over and over again. We like novelty, the challenge of upping our game, and trying something new. But we're careful not to disrupt what's working. We're cautious because we don't want to chance affecting something that already has proven results. We make sure that we're moving the right needle in the right direction.

You may take one of the amazing ideas I mention in the book and decide to build a plan around it, one that you're going to systematize. But if you don't test that against what really exists, if you don't run it by the people in your organization who understand how things currently work, you may get into trouble. Maybe you don't have enough people at your firm for the tactic to work, so the idea you latched onto might not be the best one to start with. Maybe you should start with something else, just to get some growth going, and then you can implement that when the timing is right. In other words, beware the cool idea. Just because it works in my situation, doesn't mean it'll work for you.

Stage V

MEASURE GROWTH AND EFFECTIVENESS; ADJUST AS NECESSARY

12

MEASURE THE EFFECTIVENESS OF YOUR EFFORTS

In the design of culture, it's not like you can lift a twisted pole or an unspooled reel off the production belt and immediately recognize a quality control issue. Our widget is made up of hundreds of intertwined experiences, each one affecting the other. All of the processes, practices, and events work in conjunction with one another; they create a balance.

Change one thing, or add something new into the mix, and you can throw off the entire ecosystem.

We've got to track our changes and measure all of their results by way of the grid because this culture-building, motivation-triggering stuff is a constant experiment with lots of variables.

Because we've got to constantly look for new and innovative ways to feed our people, build on success, and create homeostasis, we can't just—and I know I've said this many times before—set it and forget it. We've got to toy with an endless loop. This works, wait, this got broken, this thing did that but also did this, which may not be so good . . . then, making some new adjustments, we've got to let the assembly line run for another quarter and then judge *those* changes. Once again, we'll tweak the line, oil the gears, and check the product coming off the back end. We'll go through the exact quality control process that we spelled out in Chapter 10. Again. And again. And again.

Don't forget what these motivating experiences are all about: stirring the desire to go above and beyond the call of duty for some perceived reward. We want our people out there killing it and making serious strides in their career. We want everybody in our organization engaged in the culture so they'll stick around.

Stripping away the secondary gains, it would be fair to say that we're focusing on creating an engaged culture, motivating our people, because we want to make more money at the end of the day and enjoy our lives, the majority of which is spent at work. It's easy enough to tell if you're happier at the office, subjective as that may be, but now the trick is to determine if your efforts have shown themselves in your bottom line. To see if the rubber is in fact meeting the road.

First things first: how do you know if your line-item experiences are in good working order? We assigned grades to them in Chapter 10 and noted them on the proper page of the grid, but how do you come up with the right number? How can you really tell if you're hitting the nail on the head?

A Fabulous Carrot, or Not

If you walk away from a quarter and show that a -3 on the culture grid went to a 2, and a 0 went to a 4, you can assume that your machine is in good working order. The tweak you made brought an experience into better alignment. One or more motivation types were summarily triggered. Whatever action you took was in fact a success.

Nice job.

Except, how do you know that line item merits a 5 this quarter? I mean, it's easy enough to assume that it does once you're invested in the process, but how can you be sure? That is, after all, the name of this game: being sure that what you're doing is actually satisfying the intended purpose.

Let me walk you through my thought process. Remember, I don't trust my judgment or myself as far as I can throw me. I put a system in place so I don't fool myself into thinking that I'm smarter than I look.

As I mentioned earlier, my business partner and I decided years ago to run a contest modeled off of the NCAA's March Madness. I'm not a huge basketball fan, but my partner is, and so are a lot of our advisors. We put together a grid and randomly assigned advisors to square off against each other to see who would make it to the next round. Every two weeks, the advisor who scored the most points based on submitted business, paid business, and placed business advanced to the next round. Those who didn't make it to the next round were added to the consolation grid. We kept everybody appraised through regular emails and notifications on the video screens. After a number of rounds, two advisors on each grid were left to battle it out. Having two winners from the consolation bracket, not just the advanced level bracket, kept everyone engaged the entire run. The winners of the final round walked away with a prize, the size of which didn't seem to matter. From what we could tell, our advisors really seemed to love the game.

But was March Madness working for us?

First of all, we're not going to marry ourselves to any experience, let alone March Madness. When we first thought of it, we decided to run it as a pilot program for the quarter. You can't fail a pilot, right? It's not written in stone; it's just an experiment we're going to try for three short months. Let's get that whole mindset thing out of the way so we can see with eyes wide open.

How does March Madness play out in the actual execution? Am I seeing what I envisioned?

Do I even have a vision?

We're back once again to the whole vision thing. You can't hit a target you can't see.

To better judge if we're getting the desired outcome with a new event or experience, we benchmark success even before we get started. That's your first level filter.

STEP ONE: Benchmark success

If I initiated March Madness to better impact those motivated by inclusion, to create a situation where everybody gets together and experiences the sense of being part of the team, or to better integrate the advisors with the staff so we all feel like we're working together to pull the same cart, what would success look like?

Say we have seventy-five advisors involved in the contest. If I'm not hearing fifty talking about who won the last round or who they're up against next, they might not consider the event all that compelling.

Am I hearing people commenting on the game on a regular basis, or not? That's a hard data point that can easily be gathered.

If I initiated March Madness to better impact those motivated by ego, to create a situation where everybody wants to experience the win, what would success look like?

I'd watch how people react to the scoring system. If they know they can earn a point for the most submitted business, are they suddenly hustling to that end? Are they teasing each other, egging each other on? Are they making suggestions to the new hires who can win a round against a long-standing member who may have let his or her guard down? If the players are laughing and joking, talking smack, then we're on to something. Especially if they feel compelled to consistently bring in more business just to prove they're top dog.

We've got ourselves another hard data point.

Knowing these details upfront, benchmarking them, will allow me to decide if the experience is doing the intended job, or not.

It's the upfront work, the painted picture of success that allows us to say, "Okay, if we're hearing these things, seeing these things, maybe we want to keep March Madness on the roster."

STEP TWO: Implement the experiment for a solid quarter or more

March Madness is a pilot project with a success target. We implement it for a quarter and collect the data along the way. You can go back to Chapter 10 and read more about my reasoning for this. In short: do it and don't second-guess yourself.

STEP THREE: Reconcile

When we get to the end of the quarter, we reconcile what happened. We compare the actual results against what we envisioned. Did we produce what we'd hoped? Did we hear and see what we wanted to? We give our efforts a grade relative to our benchmark.

Usually, we're looking at three options for that line item at this point: We either keep March Madness, and it becomes part of us, part of the usual course of business; we kill it because we're so far off target or it was just not the right timing for it, not the right choice; or we decide to tweak a component of it.

Just so you know, we ended up keeping March Madness. We've been running it for nine years. We've been tweaking it consistently to get more bang for the buck. For instance, because March tends to be a good month revenue-wise, we transformed March Madness into Summer Madness to capitalize on the associated revenue bump. No more summer lull.

An event is an event is an event unless it's all part of the cultural design. And that goes for axe-throwing, Happy Hour, and game night.

To download the rules of engagement and a sample bracket, head on over to **theculturejunky.com/courses**.

Judging Your Culture

Now it's time to assess your target culture, the average of all of the experiences that you've created for your people.

How do you judge a culture? Well, you've designed this culture for a number of reasons. This whole book has been about putting together an effective culture-building plan, one that's going to do an intended job, which should be made manifest in the numbers.

Let's just assume it's twelve months down the line, and you're going back and looking at your baseline indices—revenue, retention, manpower growth, and any other indices you decided need a boost. If you've been consistently experimenting, tweaking, focusing on the gaps, you're going to start seeing traction, growth. The needle will begin to move.

Go back to your baseline indices that you compiled in Chapter 2.

You set specific goals to aim for as well, so how'd you do? How do your current numbers look relative to the goals you set?

That there is pretty much how you judge a culture.

Will I see a jump in revenue at the end of twelve months? That's the single question I'm asked every time I discuss culture with one of my peers over the phone or on a barstool.

The answer in short: if you follow the process, step-by-step, you will see results. If you refrain from short-cut taking, you systematize, you measure, and you stop throwing random darts at random walls, you're going to see massive improvement. You're going to have yourself a sticky culture and a line of ideal candidates banging on your door.

Now, we're dialing up the thermostat, so it takes a while for the pilot to kick on. So, you've got to buck up and practice patience.

It took us years to get to where we are now—to become who we are now. You may have to rotate this thing for quite some time, try this practice and then that one, until you've built a series of systems that produce the exact experience you want. And I'll remind you: the experiences you create have to support your desired culture, not mine. In no way am I saying, "Look at my culture. Repeat what I've done, and you'll be great." Because I don't think that's remotely right.

If your starting culture is an absolute disaster, it's going to be easier to move the needle because there are so many pieces that have no doubt been ignored. Seeing the component pieces for what they are is half the battle.

If you've got two leaders out there doing the hiring, just equipping them with a few systematized practices designed to make the right people happy will allow them to immediately get better results. They'll be saying and doing stuff that seriously attracts potential candidates. You'll see an uptick in manpower growth sooner than you'd think.

How that translates into revenue depends.

If I were to hire somebody today who's currently working in the industry where I'm not slowed down by the licensing requirements, I might not see a dollar for a quarter. If I've got to onboard a new hire, integrate him, it may be three, four months until he starts producing revenue and the dollars hit my bottom line.

Just so you know my take: I'm in it for the long haul. I'm just trying to move the needle and grow every year.

Keep the experiment going. Look at the variables. Tweak this one, then that one, and see what happens to the end result. Look at the indices at the end of each quarter from there on in. Pay attention to those the way you do your culture grid. Because they are, in fact, intertwined.

Exercise 12.1: Measure Against the Original Company Baseline

Go back to your baseline indices. Fill in your numbers at the twelve-month mark. (We're jumping ahead to the one-year mark, but notice that once you've gotten the hang of this, you could and should be measuring every quarter.) See if the things that you've been doing are affecting the bottom line. The numbers don't lie.

How do those numbers compare to the target you set? What did you want your revenue to be in twelve months? Your manpower growth? Whatever it was you wanted to improve upon by working on your culture, is the increase a good indication that you're going in the right direction? Are the actions you've taken to build culture yielding the right results?

13

A WRENCH IN
THE GEARS

While I was finishing up the final draft of this book, the COVID-19 pandemic shut down the world. Welcome to tough times. People had been losing their jobs right and left, the stock markets had taken a tumble, and folks had to figure out how to navigate a whole new world.

Instead of falling apart like so many other companies you read about in the papers, however, business for us was booming. Recruiting had gone nuts. Manpower was at an all-time high, which is how we win this particular game.

My peers were all freaking out. I know because I was on the phone with them more than ever. They had no idea how they were going to navigate the shit storm.

Let me explain the difference between our two separate experiences.

I read an article that claimed that we could expect an increase in breakups during and after the pandemic. Divorce lawyers could count on being busier than ever. That's because a light had suddenly shined on our relationships. Once we had slowed down, we could actually see who we were "married" to.

The folks who were beating down my door for an interview had suddenly realized who and what they were married to business-wise. It also occurred to them that, given the chaos, now was the perfect time to pivot and make a change.

Most of my peers had simply hit the pause button on their culture-building activities because they were in sheer reactive mode. "What we need to do," they said, "is make sure we've got money coming in." So the last thing they were thinking about was the need to create experiences.

Except, think of how that played out for their people who were freaking out, too.

It's as though their company had suddenly abandoned them, jerked from underneath them the warm-and-fuzzies that kept them attached to the raft.

That's probably part of the reason we're talking to so many people now, not just because their own lives got disrupted and they're taking a good hard look at reality, but also because no one is responding to their needs.

The moment we recognized that we were dealing with a long-term issue, my partner gathered our advisors and addressed their concerns. He held a series of town hall Zoom meetings and came up with a pro-active plan to deal with the new constraints.

Then, he and with the culture grids in hand got to work.

"Okay," I said, "let's go top to bottom on every single impact point that we have, every single experience we create for our people, and let's adjust the ones we need to for this environment."

Take the presentation of business cards line item. Based on the work from home environment, obviously I can't go and sit down with a new hire at his desk and have this whole great experience where I present him with his new cards in a special case. We can't even hand him the cards in the hall or put them in his mailbox the way we once did. Now, our culture director has them shipped to the new hire. Knowing the shipping arrival date, she then sets up a Zoom call so I can have that conversation with him virtually. We can create the same experience with just a small change.

Twenty minutes later, we looked at each other and agreed that we had a way to do everything that we'd done before. In other words, we successfully pivoted.

How we specifically do any one thing isn't the point of the exercise. It's the destination we're after, which is our target culture. The drive to that destination doesn't have to change at all. We just have to take a few detours to get around the roadblocks. After a few small adjustments, our experiences remain intact, despite the new constraints.

Maybe we'll carry on with our new procedures. Maybe we'll switch things up again moving forward. Who knows what the new normal will require? With that document at hand, with our system, those kinds of adjustments aren't a big deal. They allow us to keep consistent even if we have to switch everything up again another dozen times. Twenty minutes, and the job is done.

Now, if I didn't have that document, I guarantee it would *not* have taken twenty minutes to adjust. I guarantee you we'd have missed the business cards and a bunch of other stuff, because it just wouldn't have been front of mind. Those experiences would change and who knows how that would affect the relationship with our advisors. One experience affects the other and the other, and let's not forget that culture is the average of all the experiences put together.

Shining the Light on Relationships

When did we forget that we can't abandon our pals when we're scared? That we can't suddenly bail?

When you're a kid, you hang out with your buddies, and you do some stuff that makes you feel like you're in it together through thick and thin. Half the joy is seeing how much everyone else is enjoying the shared experience. And it's those experiences that glue you together for decades to come.

How is it that we've forgotten that sense of shared pleasure as adults and business owners? The one-for-all-and-all-for-one feeling?

Worse, when did we decide that it was okay to surround ourselves with people we don't really like and make them do things they don't want to do all for the sake of . . . what? Because that's the way it's always been done? When did we forget that when everyone is all in, amazing things can happen?

This book is about recreating and maintaining that feeling for both you and your people—especially if they're of a free-agents mindset. It's about fixing what ails your organization—namely, a lack of engagement, negligible manpower growth, or the inability to retain good people or recruit someone who hasn't been around the circuit a dozen times, all of which adds up to healthy revenue. And, it's about building your culture, one that allows you to have fun, a sense of purpose and mission, and money in your pocket.

This book has provided you with the grid and the system that will allow you to manage the wrenches that get thrown into your gears. This system, this grid, is the one thing that's going to keep the shit from flying. This is what will keep you on the right track no matter what comes at you. It's the continuity plan for your culture.

But this book also offers a number of lessons I'd like to summarize here.

1. The goal is to create a culture that makes the right people want to stay.

If you don't love coming to work every day, it's your fault. Shine a light on your company culture, and the truth will be revealed. You don't have to wait for a pandemic to do this. If you're not happy, then most likely the rest of the organization is miserable, too.

Don't think for a second that misery is not impacting the bottom line. It's killing it. Happy people are productive people, and productive people are profitable people. Unhappy people cost you money, time, and energy.

That means you'll need to spend some time determining the sort of environment and people that will work well for who you are as a person. If you do that, you'll get folks in who will not only buy into you—they'll become raving fans who'll spread your story far and wide, so everyone they know begs to work for you. You'll never have to worry about recruitment again. Sure, you can get people in with resumes, but if your culture sucks, meaning it's a poor fit for them, they're just not going to stay.

Like a fishing rod you buy on Amazon, your culture should be alluring to certain kinds of people—people who share much in common with you, who want the same experience that you do, that you provide. Your culture should make certain people happy, just like you. Others it should leave cold, and that's just fine.

That means you'll have to break down what you're after in very real terms and then figure out who belongs in that environment and who doesn't. Sure, you want your culture to be comfortable, so people will stick around, but you also want it to be a culture that you'll thrive in, that's suited to your personality, to your style, to your take on the world.

2. Before you have culture, you need vision.

The problem with most organizations is that none of the leaders know what they want, let alone who they are. They know they need culture, or they might know that their culture isn't right, or that it sucks, but they have no vision for it.

What's it like, this thing you're looking to create? What are you actually going for? Give me the details; give me the specifics; paint me a really clear picture—not some half-baked, stick-figure mess. Get serious. Get down and dirty with the target.

To get at the vision for a culture, you need to look at your values as a human being and as a businessperson first. If you're going to be a happy camper at work, you're going to want the people who work with you to possess a good chunk of these qualities or values or whatever we want to call them.

The clues to who you are and what you want may also be found in your origin story. This is the story you tell others, particularly new recruits, to allow them to know who you are, what your take on work and life is, and why you do things the way you do. (If, by the way, they like your story, they'll buy into it and sell it for you every chance they get. When your people love the idea of your story—when they see themselves as being behind the story as well, as fellow heroes on the journey—that's when you know you've got yourself a cultural fit.)

What's your unique story? Where do you come from, who are you, what do you stand for? What obstacles have you overcome on your climb up the ladder? What dragons have you had to slay? How did your journey change you? What makes your struggle universal? What make it unique to you?

How might you summarize it into a culture manifesto so your people can share it as well?

If left alone, absent of strategy, culture will just show up. Most of the time, this accidental culture isn't ideal or even close to what you want.

3. You need a Red Velvet Rope Rule, one that you're willing to execute on.

I see recruitment (and retention, and engagement) as a selection problem. Bring in the right people, and you'll raise the rates, no problem. Again, that means you need to be able to describe the qualities of superstar agents and those who would be Kryptonite to your organization, and then create a hiring policy based on this information.

Executing on your Red Velvet Rope Rule once you've determined the qualities that will work for you, and which qualities will serve to destroy your culture, is fraught with problems and potential loopholes.

If you're looking to create something new, you've got to evaluate each and every advisor currently on board and decide if he or she satisfies the requirements of your evolving culture, or if you're going to need to part ways.

Right now, you may not be in a position to do anything about the advisors who fail to meet your Red Velvet Rope Rule, but, as soon as you are, you'll need to prioritize this culling. In a perfect world, you'd dump them before you begin bringing new people into your organization. In an imperfect world, you need to be shedding mismatch as you're bringing newbies into the fold if you're going to survive in this game.

Most of the I'll-wait-and-see-if-I-can-make-this-work loopholes involve big-earners. Two things can happen when you're overly dependent on whales that clearly don't fit your culture, both of which are fatal. A: Try to change anything and they'll leave. Or, B: They'll destroy the culture, particularly if they're jerks, because they'll insist on (and get) different treatment than the rest. Anybody who comes into the ecosystem will naturally revolt. And there goes your cohesion and your warm, inviting feeling.

If you don't have a strong foundation to hire into, you're going to have less dramatic results. If you haven't cleaned up your gene pool, you could have the most amazing and attractive culture compared to what you had, but that one bad apple you've got hanging around is going to squash the manpower growth results.

Everyone in your organization needs to understand your Red Velvet Rope Rule so they can act accordingly.

Our current advisors are guarding the door, only letting in others who promise to do well. Our hiring, in other words, is all culture-driven. While our current advisors have a good intuitive feel about fit, they've also been told in no uncertain terms whom we're looking to attract. They've been schooled on our Red Velvet Rope Rule, and they value the fact that we're something of an exclusive club. Your advisors are an expression and an extension of you, be you a shark or the entrepreneurial type or a micromanager. You are the company you keep. Choose your advisors as carefully as you choose your friends. Actually, choose them more carefully, because it's safe to assume that many of your advisors will become your friends.

4. Motivation is your job.

A culture is created around motivation. As a manager, your job is to generate feelings of purpose and personal growth for your advisors. What keeps this particular person motivated? That's the question you've always got to be asking yourself.

Answering those questions is how a powerful, engaging culture is born. Motivated people make money for everyone involved, and they stick around, rave about you, and share in your story. That's why culture matters.

Every experience we deliver is about motivation, understanding who we're trying to influence, and why. Your job is to uncover the biggest motivator in the lives of your people so you can paint the vision that will pull them forward, particularly when things get tough. As the owner, your job is to focus on the motivation style, so when you're working the plan for the organization at large and that of the individual advisor, you'll know how to implement; you'll know what you need to do to keep him engaged in the game.

You need to first identify your motivation gaps before you start throwing random events and practices into the mix. That's where the grid comes in. Then, on a regular basis, you need to measure these things to see if they're effective or not. If they're getting at the motivational style(s) wrapped up in the mix. Ask yourself: what's the reason for hosting an event or providing a particular experience in the first place? What specific outcome am I after?

We're looking to measure the ROI of an experience. If you can't measure it, don't do it.

5. If you want a culture, you've got to treat it like a widget.

Culture is not this touchy feely, feel-good thing, take some ideas off each other and run with it. You want a culture? You've got to treat it like a widget. You've got to train the assembly line workers, who serve as an impact point during the manufacturing process; you've got to have the right raw materials; and you've got to understand what you're trying to produce in the first place and why. That it's a manufactured good. It's repeatable, it's predictable, and there are a lot of moving parts.

You can't ignore the planning part and jump straight into action. You can't skip steps because they feel uncomfortable, irrelevant, or time-consuming, or your widgets will be all screwed up. A lack of planning is equivalent to throwing a box of mystery parts onto a conveyor belt and hoping it produces what you want.

We want to establish a baseline picture of your business as it is today so we can go back and look at what you're doing to see if it's working and if the assembly line is producing exactly what you'd hoped.

What are the metrics you're dealing with today that advertise the problem you mean to address by focusing on culture? What's the linchpin—the indicator or two—that, if improved, will allow you to solve the problem?

Then, measure the things that you're doing to create the culture you've designed. Instead of feeling impatient, approach this thing like a scientist. Going through this process, tweaking this part of the process and implementing and planning the supporting systems that keep things culturally cozy, will ensure that you get precisely the outcome that you're after.

We measure because we've got to assess the state of the widgets coming off the belt. Are we producing the right thing or not? There is no other way. Then, we've got to come up with a plan to support or to evolve your people's experiences so they stick around.

In the design of culture, there is a way to tell if you're consistently producing the experience you intended and if you're motivating your people with the proper practices and events to that end. To better judge if you're getting the desired outcome with a new experience, you benchmark success even before you get started, you listen for what's being said, you watch how it plays out on the grid, and you look for the effect on the company indices. Because, eventually, that's where all your efforts will show up.

As warm and fuzzy as culture is, at least the culture I've created, it's a machine. It's a cold, metallic machine designed to pick out experiences targeted at a result. The result being a sense of the warm and fuzzies *and* quantifiable net results.

Just like any complicated manufacturing processes rife with glitches, we can't fix everything in one quarter, because culture-building and engagement is a process. But we're after the 20 percent that will do 80 percent of the culture-building work. What constitutes the 20 percent? It's the stuff we're seriously getting wrong. The job at hand is to identify the options, to pinpoint events and experiences designed to delight your advisors, and to focus on the one (or two or three) thing(s) you're going to do consistently for this quarter. And it's not just you, the leader, who's going to do these things. And you're not just going to randomly task these things out. You're going to create a plan and get other people involved. Your job is to break it down into a workable plan and create automation.

6. Systems allow you to do your job.

You'll need to create systematized experiences to keep the individuals in your organization happy, to hit his or her motivational style where it counts. Systems are what allow for mindless execution. None of us thinks about whatever it is we planned to do; we just do it.

Culture is made up of the little things, because little things are the big things, which is another reason you need to think in terms of systems. You know what happens when you've got a million little things to do. Something vital always falls off the plate.

The only reason implementation happens consistently in my firm is because there's a system that's pushing out a product every single day.

Every second, I've got at least a dozen people tied into that system.

A system requires that you assign members of your team with owning a tactic, new process, or event and decide who's going to be responsible for the various pieces of it. You identify the players for that piece, for that system, and then you discuss the outcome you're looking for with your team.

Every single place you touch, talk to, market to, or integrate with an advisor should be documented on the culture grid. That way, you can continually judge each impact point. Examine every single event or experience that creates an interaction, all those places where your advisors intersect with the service side of the firm. You need to know them all and keep score of them all, because, remember, culture is not an event, practice, or experience; it's the average of them all. By now you should be able to repeat that mantra in your sleep.

Look at your people as an average; measure your efforts against the entire population. Yes, you should be interested in the individuals, but the sum of the individuals is the ecosystem.

You'll need to do this evaluation over and over again so you can keep the ecosystem in line with your vision. Your documentation should be based on both the things you want to hear and see and the things you don't want to hear and see, all of which are based on the experience you want to create. The grid helps you identify the gaps in your culture-building efforts and create plans to attack them. That grid allows you to assess the lay of the land quickly, no matter what the level of disarray.

My thesis is simple: your people are your power. They comprise the personality of your organization. They not only make or break your bottom line—they color nearly every waking moment of your work-day, if not your life.

Surround yourself with near-strangers, or blowhards, or whiners, or the perpetually unhappy, and you're going to count the days until you can make just enough money to bag the rat race. And life's too short to live like that.

Any leader has the ability to completely transform his or her environment. Most, however, react to the very human workplace by allowing it to squash them or leave them indifferent. Sure, building culture is all the rage; most leaders say they want to improve their culture. Again, if 25 percent of all North American companies have a culture plan, I'm betting 5 percent of that total implement that plan properly and then get *any* kind of result. Wanting something and doing what it takes to get it are two completely different things.

You've got in your hands the blueprint to build a culture that will make you happy and rich. The process I've outlined within this book will get you there, but you need to be patient. This culture-building stuff takes time. You'll never be able to set it and forget it because it, like you, will continually evolve over time.

I raise a beer to you. Here's to slipping past the old guards and creating an outrageously good experience for all involved.